A GARDENER'S GUIDE TO

Flowering shrubs

Editor John Negus
Series Editor Graham Strong

INDEX

CONTENTS

GUIDE TO PLANT SHAPES
These diagrams are used on each page to give a quick guide to the
shape of the mature plant.

*LEFT: There are few more captivating early spring sights in a
woodland glade than a marriage of azaleas and chalice-flowered
magnolias.*

GROWING FLOWERING SHRUBS

Beautiful borders can be created almost entirely from shrubs – the bones of a garden. They impart form and character and complement trees and herbaceous perennials. All shrubs flower – and many that have small, modest flowers produce bright berries that ornament the late summer, autumn and winter garden.

Shrubs are usually defined as perennial woody plants. They are frequently multi-stemmed, but not always, and the line between tall shrubs and small trees is rather vague. Indeed, gardeners and professional horticulturists do not always agree. Shrubs may be evergreen or deciduous, leaves are small or large, glossy or matt and come in a huge range of shapes. Some shrubs, such as hibiscus, have showy flowers. Others, such as box, have tiny, insignificant ones. Cotton lavender (*santolina*) and rosemary, among others, have aromatic foliage. A few – such as syringa, mock orange and choisya – are prized for their sweetly perfumed blooms.

Shrubs come in every shape and size. There is a species or variety to suit virtually every situation. When you are planning a garden, select kinds that favour a particular position. Will the shrub thrive in full sun, or does it prefer shade? Consider how high and wide it will grow. Some shrubs can take up to 5–10 years to mature, become well established and assume their final shape. Never buy a large-growing shrub for a small space, thinking you can prune it to keep it small. Repeated cutting back will spoil its natural symmetry and you will eventually come to hate it and thus remove it.

ABOVE: *Brilliant red 'Royal William' – a bounteous Large Flowered rose.*

LEFT: *A sculpturally appealing symphony of golden pansies, box hedging and green bottlebrush blooms of* Euphorbia wulfenii.

PROPAGATION

Most shrubs are raised from stem cuttings. They may be grown from soft-tip cuttings (of, for example, hydrangea or fuchsia) taken in late spring and early summer; semi-ripe nodal cuttings of side shoots, or heel cuttings of shoots tugged from the main stem in midsummer – most shrubs being propagated this way; or from dormant hardwood cuttings of deciduous shrubs.

Soft-tip, semi-ripe nodal and heel cuttings should be 5–10cm (2–4in) long and taken from strong, healthy plants, preferably from stems that have not flowered. Hardwood cuttings of mature, dormant shoots, 25–30cm (10–12in) long, are rooted in autumn, in a slit trench in the garden. Layering, that is, pegging down young, flexible stems close to the soil any time between spring and autumn, is another easy way to multiply shrubs.

Soft-tip and semi-ripe nodal cuttings

Take these early in the day, when plump and dew-fresh. If you are not able to insert them into pots of compost immediately, enclose them in a plastic bag and keep them in a cool, shady place.

Use a very sharp knife or razor blade to remove all but the topmost two or three leaves. If the leaves are large, as in hydrangeas, it is best to shorten them by half their length. At the base of the cutting make a clean, horizontal cut, just below a node (joint) from which leaves appear. Encourage rapid rooting by dipping the cutting in hormone rooting compound. Prepare a rooting mix of three parts, by volume, of coarse, washed sand or Perlite and one part of peat or loam-based seed compost. Alternatively, use proprietary, peat-based cutting compost. Place the compost mix in a small, 10cm (4in) pot and gently firm it. Make holes with a pencil where the cuttings are to go and insert them to a third of their length, about 5cm (2in) apart.

Firm compost around the stems. You can place several cuttings in one pot. Water them in, allow compost to drain, then transfer them to a propagator or garden frame, or enclose them in an inflated plastic bag and place them on a windowsill. In warm conditions, soft-tip cuttings will root within 2–4 weeks. You can tell if a cutting has rooted if new leaves have formed and a gentle pull on the stem meets with resistance. A few weeks later, move the plant into a small pot of potting compost.

HARDWOOD CUTTINGS

They usually take many weeks or months to root. Leaves may form long before roots develop. They should be about 30cm (12in) long and 6–13mm (¼–½in) thick. Take them from the middle of well-ripened, current-year shoots. Prepare them by making a gently sloping cut just above the topmost bud and a horizontal cut immediately below the bottom node (joint). Next, in a sunny, well-drained area of deeply dug and friable soil, use a spade to take out a 15–20cm (6–8in) deep trench with one vertical wall. Trickle a 2.5cm (1in) layer of sharp sand into it.

Insert cuttings to two-thirds their depth, 15cm (6in) apart, pressing them into the sand. Tread soil firmly around them, hoe out footprints and water copiously.

Refirm cuttings in winter when hard frost lifts them. Roots will form in spring. By autumn, plants will be ready for moving to where you wish to display them.

Some roses will grow quite readily from cuttings, but others will not grow vigorously on their own roots. Commercial nurseries 'bud' rose varieties on to rootstocks of wild or species roses. (Budding is a form of grafting using dormant leaf buds.)

LAYERING

Take out a 15cm (6in) hole next to the plant and remove any leaves that might be buried, from the selected shoot. Make a sloping, 4cm (1½in) cut through a joint in the middle of the shoot and wedge open the cut with a matchstick. Half fill the hole with a mix of equal parts sharp sand and soil and then peg the cut part of the shoot into it. Cover the shoot with more of the same mix and tie the exposed end to a cane to keep it upright. Water the layer to settle the soil around it and place a large, flat stone over it to keep the soil damp.

About a year later, when roots have formed, sever the new shrub, or layer, from its parent by cutting the stem of the parent shrub where it enters the ground. Then leave your new shrub *in situ* or transplant it to a new position in the garden.

Some shrubs may be grown from seed, but only the species will produce plants that match their parent.

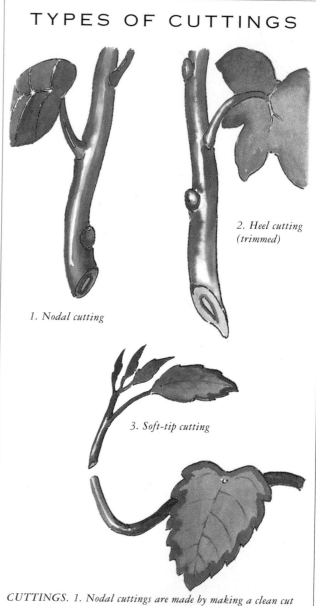

TYPES OF CUTTINGS

2. Heel cutting (trimmed)

1. Nodal cutting

3. Soft-tip cutting

CUTTINGS. 1. Nodal cuttings are made by making a clean cut 3mm (⅛in) below a node (joint). 2. Heel cuttings are tugged from the main stem, to leave a tag of bark, which is trimmed back close to the base of the shoot. 3. Soft-tip cuttings are made from young, green shoot tips. Remove lower leaves (as here) before inserting in compost.

CHOOSING A PLANT

When choosing plants at a garden centre, the biggest is not always the best. Look for those that are well shaped and have a good cover of healthy leaves. Avoid plants that have woody roots protruding from drainage holes, those that are excessively tall for the pot and those that have knobbly, thickened stem bases. All these features show that the plant is pot-bound and that it should have been moved into a larger container some time ago. All plants suffer from some degree of transplanting shock, but the smaller the plant the less traumatic the move. Ideally, select plants in bloom to ensure that you are getting the colour and variety you want.

SOIL PREPARATION

Because most shrubs are fairly long-lived and form a garden's permanent framework, it is worth putting in a bit of time and effort into preparing a good home for them and thus protect your investment. Shrubs planted in suitable conditions will become established more quickly, and their healthy growth will be less vulnerable to attack by pests and disease than plants that are treated more hastily.

Few shrubs tolerate heavy, waterlogged soil. If drainage is poor, you may need to consider raising the planting area or installing subsoil drains. Heavy, clay soils can be improved by adding gypsum at the rate of 200–300g per square metre (7–11oz per sq yd) and by working in large quantities of well-rotted, organic material. Organic matter should be dug in several weeks ahead of planting. Sandy soils, in which water and nutrients are quickly lost, benefit greatly from the addition of large amounts of organic matter before planting. All plants and soils are better for being mulched with humus-forming, well-rotted animal manure, compost, leaf mould, straw or decayed grass clippings, as these not only retain moisture in the soil but also keep the soil and plants well nourished. Mulches should only be laid on moist soil.

STRIKING SOFT-TIP CUTTINGS

1. TO TAKE A CUTTING, gather shoots when dew-fresh and place in a plastic bag. Prepare stems by trimming to length and cutting just below a node (joint). Keep cuttings cool and shaded. Remove lower leaves, which will rot if buried.

2. FILL A SMALL POT, which has plenty of drainage holes, with gritty cutting compost. Use a pencil to make holes for inserting cuttings to half their length. Firm compost around them.

3. WATER IN CUTTINGS well, but gently, taking care not to dislodge them. They should not need watering again until new growth indicates that roots have formed. If you are unsure of how dry the compost is, and the pot feels light, add just a little water.

4. MAKE A WIRE OR BAMBOO FRAME that fits inside the pot and is tall enough to clear cuttings. Place a plastic bag over the frame and secure it to the pot. The bag will keep air and soil moist. Root cuttings in good light but not direct sunlight.

Framed by statuesque conifers and a fiery, autumn-hued tree, crimson-flowered Hebe 'Great Orme' *makes a fine focal point beside this gravel path. Usefully, this evergreen shrub starts blooming in July but seldom finishes before late October.*

PLANTING

With good soil preparation and correct planting techniques your shrubs should flourish. Most container-grown shrubs are transplanted throughout the year, provided the soil is crumbly and workable and frost is not forecast. In winter, in gardens prone to hard frost, it is best to transplant only dormant, deciduous plants.

Bare-rooted shrubs, usually deciduous, are planted when leaves have fallen – from autumn to early spring.
• Check that the position chosen for your shrub will allow it to develop full height and spread without your having to cut it back. You should also cater for its other needs: soil type – heavy or light, warm and free-draining – and sun or shade.
• Dig a hole at least twice as wide as the plant's root system and about the same depth. Loosen soil in the bottom of the hole and around the sides. If it is clayey, work in grit or gravel to avoid creating a sump in which roots may drown.
• Do not put fresh manure into the hole. Instead, mix a balanced fertiliser, such as fish, blood and bone meal, Growmore or a slow-release brand, with soil you firm around the roots. Roots must not come into direct contact with fertiliser, which may burn them.
• If you are planting a container-grown shrub bought in a stiff plastic pot, thoroughly water the compost to loosen any roots clinging to the pot sides. Invert the plant and gently tap its pot rim on a hard surface so that the rootball slides out. Carefully tease out compacted, encircling roots from the rootball.
• Trim away any roots that are damaged.
• Place the plant in its hole, at the same depth that it was previously growing. Lay a cane over the hole, next to the plant, to check this. Backfill the hole with soil that you have dug out and tread the soil firmly around the rootball. Do not tread on the rootball itself.
• Water in thoroughly to remove any air pockets and settle the soil around the feeding root hairs.
• Mulch the root area, but keep mulch well clear of the stem, because its bark could rot. Organic mulches, such as manures and composts, help to condition soil and feed plants. They break down and disappear after a year or so, so replace them annually.

MAINTENANCE

Water newly planted shrubs regularly and copiously, specially in droughty weather until they are well established.

Re-feed autumn-planted shrubs in spring, and spring planted in summer, by topdressing (sprinkling) the root area with a complete plant food. Fish, blood and bone meal or pelleted poultry manure is ideal for most shrubs, but avoid using poultry manure on lime-hating rhododendrons and summer-flowering heathers, among others.

PRUNING

Many shrubs will never need shoots removing unless you wish to rejuvenate very old plants or take out wayward stems. If you wish to cut back a spring-flowering plant, prune it when its blooms fade. The only exception to this is plants, such as firethorn and cotoneaster, that are grown for their berries. Shrubs, such as *Buddleja davidii*, that flower from mid- to late summer are best pruned the following spring.

To train a single-stemmed standard, select a young shrub with a straight stem and shorten laterals (side shoots) to within 2.5cm (1in) of the trunk. These leafy stumps help to conduct sap to the head of the standard. If the main stem is slender – it usually is – you may need to tie it to a cane. As the stem lengthens, shorten further side shoots to an inch or so until the stem is as high as required – normally 1.2–1.8m (4–6ft). Then, when the head is developing well, trim it to a ball shape and cut off side shoots flush with the stem.

HARDINESS

All plants mentioned flourish outdoors, apart from frost-tender ardisia, echium, oleander, plumbago, pomegranate and heliotrope, which are normally overwintered in a greenhouse or conservatory and moved to a sheltered, sunny place for summer. Of the relatively hardy kinds, some in very cold, windswept or frost-pocket gardens may need tucking up for winter. The best way to protect them is to cover them with an open-topped wigwam of bubble plastic or several layers of fibre fleece. Make sure the material does not touch the leaves or stems, or, if moist, it might rot them.

WHAT CAN GO WRONG?

Yellow leaves
- Plants have been overwatered or are too dry.
- Plants may need feeding: fertilise the plant with a high-nitrogen tonic if this has not been done for two or three months and see if there is any improvement within the next two or three weeks.
- Older leaves may turn bright yellow before dropping. Do not worry; they have finished their useful life.
- When new leaves on azaleas are pale yellow yet the veins are green, they probably require a dose of iron chelates, which aids chlorophyll production. Apply this in spring and early summer, carefully following the manufacturer's directions on the label.

Curled or distorted leaves
- Look for aphids (greenfly) – tiny, sticky, reddish-brown, grey or green, sap-sucking insects clustering on new growth. Control them with an insecticide containing pirimicarb, permethrin, biollethrin, horticultural soap, rotenone or pyrethrins. Spray at dusk when bees and other beneficial insects have retired for the night. Avoid spraying when it is hot, too, because foliage may be scorched by high temperatures.
- Some viruses manifest themselves this way and there is no cure. Consult reference books or experts to see if your plant has succumbed to one of these diseases. If affected, dig it up and burn it.
- Check that there has been no drift of any herbicide from nearby spraying. Even very small amounts of spray drift, especially from selective lawn weedkillers, can distort leaves of very sensitive plants, such as tomatoes and roses.

Black spots on leaves
- These may be fungal leaf spots. On roses, they are probably caused by black spot, a common disease that badly blotches leaves. Control it by spraying with bupirimate with triforine, penconazole or myclobutanil. Ideally, improve air circulation around plants and avoid wetting leaves when watering, which should not be done late in the day. Large, brownish-black spots on camellias probably resulted from sunburn.

Greyish-white powder on leaf surfaces
- This deposit is probably powdery mildew, which affects a wide range of plants. Roses, azaleas, hydrangeas and many other shrubs are prone to this disease. Avoid watering late in the day and spray plants with bupirimate with triforine, myclobutanil, sulphur or penconazole. It is worse on wall shrubs in dry areas where air does not freely circulate.

Mottled leaves
- This is usually associated with sap-sucking insects such as scale, thrip, lace bug and red spider mite, which is not a true insect. Stressed, rather than healthy, plants are more liable to be attacked by these insects. Plants may be stressed by drought or overwatering, or by simply growing them away from their favoured aspect.
- Limpet-like scale insects come in various sizes and colours. Control small infestations by using a damp cloth to wipe them off leaves and stems. Eradicate severe infestations by spraying plants with malathion
- Thrips and lace bugs may be reduced by hosing the underside of leaves or by spraying with pyrethrins, malathion, pirimiphos-methyl, permethrin or insecticidal soap.
- In hot, dry weather, red spider mite can be a problem on shrubs growing in rain-sheltered spots, such as under the house eaves. Hosing the foliage helps to keep them down and obviate the need for spraying. If you have to resort to insecticides, malathion, bifenthrin and pirimiphos-methyl are effective.

Holes in leaves or on leaf margins
- This may be snail or slug damage. Snails often lurk high up on the foliage. Baiting is not effective in this instance, so pick off and kill pests. Eradicate the ground-hugging tribe by sprinkling blue-dyed molluscicide pellets containing metaldehyde or methiocarb, thinly around susceptible, soft-stemmed plants. Alternatively, ring them with grit.
- Caterpillars also chew leaves. Tackle them by hand picking or biologically controlling them with *Bacillus thuringiensis*. Effective insecticides include permethrin, bifenthrin and pirimiphos-methyl.

Stems and leaves webbed or matted together
- Webbing caterpillars, such as those of the lackey moth, can cover buds and new shoots and extensively defoliate trees and shrubs. Pull out the webbing with a gloved hand or cut out the damaged section. Spray with permethrin, bifenthrin or pirimiphos-methyl, or control the pest biologically with *Bacillus thuringiensis*. Inspect shrubs several times a year to control this pest in its early stages.

Sooty mould (a dry, black coating on leaf surfaces)
- A fungus, sooty mould feeds on sticky honeydew secreted by sap-sucking insects, such as aphids and scales. Once the pest is controlled, the mould will gradually disappear. Hosing helps. Wipe large-leaved plants with a damp cloth.

Sudden death of plant
- If leaves turn brown but remain attached to the plant, the plant has probably died from root rot. Root systems may have been damaged by excessive watering – from rain or irrigation – quite some time before the plant expires, especially in cool weather. When plants are stressed by extreme heat or wind, damaged root systems cannot cope and death follows quickly.
- If a plant is suffering from drought, its leaves may be brown and rapidly drop when watered.

Pomegranate fruits may appear in a warm garden.

ABELIA
Abelia

Abelia's pretty pink flowers appear at the end of summer. Striking, red calyces prolong the display.

An informal abelia hedge adds a little magic to a sunny and sheltered garden, Trim it lightly in spring.

FEATURES

Semi-evergreen and vigorous in mild districts, *Abelia* x *grandiflora* makes a dashing statement and a fine flowering hedge. From July to September, its arching shoots, clad with small, oval, pointed leaves, 1.2–1.5m (4–5ft) long, are sleeved with showy heads of tubular, pale pink flowers with reddish calyces. The decorative calyx persists into late autumn. 'Francis Mason' is a stunning variety with golden-variegated leaves that complement a wealth of pink blossom. Other prized kinds are lilac-pink *A. chinensis* 'Edward Goucher' and rosy-lilac *A. schumannii*.

ABELIA AT A GLANCE

Sporting clusters of pink or lilac flowers from late summer to autumn, it needs a sheltered position. Hardy to -10ºC (14ºF).

		RECOMMENDED VARIETIES
JAN	/	
FEB	/	*A. chinensis* 'Edward
MAR	prune	Goucher'
APR	plant, prune	*A.* x *grandiflora*
MAY	plant	*A.* x *grandiflora* 'Francis
JUNE	plant	Mason'
JULY	plant, flower	*A. schumannii*
AUG	plant, flower	
SEPT	plant, flower	
OCT	/	
NOV	/	
DEC	/	

CONDITIONS

Aspect Thriving in full sun and tolerating very light shade, abelia is best planted against a sheltered, south- or west-facing wall.

Site Abelia prospers in a wide range of well-drained soils, from clay-loam to sand. Enrich rapid-draining, chalky and sandy soils with well-rotted and moisture-conserving, bulky organic materials.

GROWING METHOD

Feeding Topdress the root area with bone meal in spring and autumn to encourage sturdy growth and profuse blooms.
Water freely after planting and mulch thickly with old manure, bark, cocoa shell or rotted garden compost to keep roots cool and active.

Propagation Take soft-tip cuttings in late spring and semi-ripe cuttings from mid- to late summer.

Problems Shoots are brittle and easily snapped, so be careful when pruning and planting.

PRUNING

Flowers form on current-year shoots. Once mature, keep it youthful by cutting out a third of its oldest branches in spring.

ABUTILON
Abutilon vitifolium

In a sheltered, sunny spot, Abutilon vitifolium *becomes a glowing sentinel of saucer-shaped, pale to deep mauve blooms in early summer.*

Plant award-winning 'Canary Bird' in a fertile, sun-soaked spot and enjoy a summer-long succession of pendent blooms.

FEATURES

There are few more exhilarating, summer sights than a mature shrub of *Abutilon vitifolium* festooned with white to purple-blue, saucer-shaped blooms. Studding stems clothed with three- to five-lobed, soft, grey, hairy leaves are flowers that have you looking closely at them. Making an upright 'obelisk' to around 4.5m (15ft), this shrub is worth a little cosseting – as are its eye-catching varieties, mauve-flowered 'Veronica Tennant' and 'Tennant's White'.

Closely related *A. x suntense*, a fast-growing hybrid to 3.6m (12ft), rewards us with pendent, white to violet-blue 'saucers'. Choice forms of this hybrid are purple-blue 'Geoffrey Gorer', white 'Gorer's White', deep mauve 'Jermyns' and dark violet-blue 'Violetta'. Look out, too, for 'Canary Bird', whose radiant lemon-yellow blooms illuminate a border.

ABUTILON AT A GLANCE

Loosely branched, deciduous shrub sleeved with saucer-shaped, white, blue or purple blooms in summer. Hardy to 0°C (32°F).

		RECOMMENDED VARIETIES
JAN	/	
FEB	/	*A. x suntense*
MAR	/	'Geoffrey Gorer'
APR	plant, prune	'Gorer's White'
MAY	plant	'Jermyns'
JUNE	flower, plant	'Ralph Gould'
JULY	flower, prune	'Violetta'
AUG	plant	*A. vitifolium* 'Tennant's White'
SEPT	plant	*A. vitifolium* 'Veronica Tennant'
OCT	/	
NOV	/	
DEC	/	

CONDITIONS

Aspect Position all varieties in full sun where shoots grow stocky and are massed with bloom. Make sure abutilon is sheltered from shoot-killing, icy winds.

Site This shrub tolerates a wide range of well-drained soils, but for the best results enrich the planting area with plenty of crumbly organic matter.

GROWING METHOD

Feeding For the strongest shoots and bounteous blossom, topdress the root area with fish, blood and bone meal or Growmore in spring and midsummer.
Water young plants regularly and mulch them with bulky organics to keep soil cool.
In long, dry spells, take out a moat around the plant and fill it repeatedly with water. When subsoil is soaked, replace excavated soil and cover with moisture-conserving mulch.

Propagation Increase favoured varieties from semi-ripe cuttings from mid- to late summer. *A. vitifolium* produces masses of fertile seed.

Problems Control aphids colonising soft stems by spraying with pirmicarb, pyrethrins or insecticidal soap. Leaves may be damaged by caterpillars and other chewing insects. If damage is slight, ignore it. If severe, control these pests biologically with *Bacillus thuringiensis*, or apply rotenone or pirimiphos-methyl.

PRUNING

Keep bushes compact and packed with flowering shoots by cutting back dead or dying stems to healthy growth in mid-spring. In early summer, shorten flowered stems to two-thirds their length.

SILVER WATTLE
Acacia dealbata

Silver wattle's ferny, silvery-green leaves are appealing all year round, specially if shoots are fan-trained against a warm wall.

There are few more riveting sights in a sheltered garden in early spring than Acacia dealbata *in full flower.*

FEATURES

There are around 900 species of wattle but only *Acacia dealbata* is sufficiently hardy for planting outdoors in mild districts. Rapidly growing to around 3.6m (12ft), its soft shoots are richly and appealingly clothed with ferny and silvery-sheened, evergreen leaves.

In April, year-old shoots are thickly clustered with small, double pompoms of fragrant, bright yellow blossom.

Ideally, because several days of temperatures hovering around freezing point may kill shoots, it is best fan-trained against a warm, south-facing wall.

Only in relatively frost-free districts can you successfully grow it as a free-standing shrub in the open garden. Elsewhere, set it in a large pot or tub and grow it in a conservatory, moving it outdoors into the open garden only for summer.

SILVER WATTLE AT A GLANCE

An evergreen, tender tree with silvery, ferny leaves and bobbles of yellow flowers in spring. Hardy to 0°C (32°F).

JAN	/	RECOMMENDED VARIETIES
FEB	flower	
MAR	flower	*A. dealbata*
APR	plant, flower	
MAY	prune, plant	
JUNE	plant	
JULY	plant	
AUG	plant	
SEPT	plant	
OCT	/	
NOV	/	
DEC	/	

CONDITIONS

Aspect Choose a warm, sunny site, ideally very sheltered and facing south or south-west, where it will not be exposed to leaf-blackening easterly or northerly winds.

Site Any well-drained, lime-free soil suits it. Fortify thin, sandy or gravelly soils with bulky, humus-enriching manure or well-rotted garden compost. Aerate heavy clay by working in plenty of grit or shingle. Alternatively, if puddles lie, dig a 45cm (18in) drainage trench, leading to a soakaway, and fill it with gravel or rubble to within 20cm (8in) of the soil surface.

GROWING METHOD

Feeding Encourage robust growth by annually sprinkling blood, fish and bone meal or Growmore over the rooting area in April and July. Water young plants regularly, especially in droughty spells, to help them develop a good, questing root system. Acacia appreciates occasional deep watering.

Propagation Increase acacia from semi-ripe cuttings in midsummer. Also grow from seed. Speed germination by soaking seeds overnight in hot water to soften the seed coat. Sow directly.

Problems Fortunately, it is seldom attacked by sap-sucking pests or caterpillars. If aphids cluster on shoots and cripple them, control them with pirimicarb, horticultural soap or permethrin.

PRUNING

No regular pruning is necessary. In spring, shorten any stems killed by frost back to healthy side shoots. If acacia outgrows its situation, reduce wayward stems by up to two-thirds in late spring.

CORAL BERRY
Ardisia crenata

Fetching when enhancing a patio in summer, or conservatory in winter, ardisia is famed for its large clusters of scarlet berries.

A choice, compact evergreen, ardisia's panoply of white flowers in summer prelude a bounteous display of fruits.

FEATURES

Frost-sensitive, this evergreen shrub, clothed with attractive, rounded, toothed and glossy, leathery leaves, has much to commend it. Coveted for its sprays of small, white, summer flowers, followed by a fetching and long-lasting display of bright red berries, it is easy to manage. Seldom more than 90cm (3ft) high and across, it is normally grown in a large pot and confined to a frost-free conservatory in which temperatures are at least 10°C (20°F) above freezing. In early summer when frosts finish, ardisia can be moved to highlight a lightly shaded patio.

CORAL BERRY AT A GLANCE

Sculptural evergreen with glossy leaves. White, summer flowers are followed by bright scarlet berries. Hardy to 10°C (50°F).

		RECOMMENDED VARIETIES
JAN	/	
FEB	/	*A. crenata*
MAR	/	
APR	plant, prune	
MAY	plant	
JUN	plant	
JULY	flower	
AUG	flower	
SEPT	flower	
OCT	/	
NOV	/	
DEC	/	

CONDITIONS

Aspect   Outdoors, ardisia prefers a shaded to semi-shaded position sheltered from strong winds. Indoors, from early autumn to late spring, display it in a lightly shaded conservatory.

Site   Help it excel by setting it in a large pot of John Innes potting compost No. 3. Based on moisture-retentive loam, it reduces the need for watering and encourages robust growth.

GROWING METHOD

Feeding   Encourage lustrous leaves and bounteous flowers and fruits by feeding weekly with a high-potash liquid fertiliser from spring to late summer. Alternatively, add a slow-release fertiliser to the compost in spring and replace it a year later. Water regularly from spring to autumn to keep the compost nicely moist, but ease up from autumn to winter when growth is slower. Cease feeding too.

Propagation   Take soft-tip cuttings in spring or summer.
Problems   Plants are occasionally attacked by sap-sucking scale insects, which cling like limpets to stems and leaves. Control them by spraying with malathion. Well-grown plants are seldom troubled by pests.

PRUNING

Ardisia is neat and symmetrical and cutting back is not normally necessary. If it grows too large, shorten stems to side shoots in spring.

BARBERRY
Berberis thunbergii

Berberis thunbergii *'Atropurpurea' glows with sunset hues in autumn.*

Berberis stenophylla *brightens spring with a globe of yellow blossom. Keep it youthful by shearing off faded blooms in late spring.*

FEATURES

A huge, easy family of evergreen and deciduous species and varieties, berberis will grow almost anywhere. Small bushes enhance a rock garden; larger kinds light up a border or form a burglar-proof hedge.The most popular leaf-shedding kind is *Berberis thunbergii*. A dense, rounded shrub to about 1.5m (5ft) high and across, it is armed with long, sharp spines. Long-lived, with small, bright yellow flowers that sleeve slender, whippy stems and cheer spring, its leaves turn scarlet in autumn. Bright red berries are a winter feature. Reddish-purple-leaved *B. thunbergii*

'Atropurpurea' becomes a firebrand in October. Other choice varieties of *B. thunbergii* ideal for small gardens are golden-leaved 'Aurea', purple-blackish-leaved 'Dart's Red Lady' and 'Harlequin'. Fetching, evergreen kinds are *B.* × *stenophylla* and *B. candidula*.

CONDITIONS

Aspect	Very hardy. Deciduous kinds especially resist icy winds. Berberis needs full sun to flower and fruit freely, but will tolerate light shade.
Site	Berberis prospers on a wide range of soils, from sand to heavy, often waterlogged clay.

GROWING METHOD

Feeding	Work bone meal into the root area in autumn. Water copiously and regularly in the first year after planting, to encourage good growth. Thereafter, little watering is necessary.
Propagation	Layer shoots from spring to autumn, or take semi-ripe cuttings from early to mid-autumn.
Problems	Control rust disease by spraying with a proprietary spray.

PRUNING

Bushes:	Apart from cutting back frost-damaged shoots in May, no regular pruning is needed. Renew old gaunt bushes by cutting back a third of the older stems to near ground level in April.
Hedges:	Trim when blooms fade in spring.

BARBERRY AT A GLANCE

Undemanding shrubs – many have fiery autumn leaf tints – bearing yellow or orange spring flowers. Hardy to -25ºC (-13ºF).

JAN	/	RECOMMENDED VARIETIES
FEB	/	
MAR	plant	Deciduous
APR	flower, prune	*B. thunbergii*
MAY	flower, plant	*B. thunbergii* 'Atropurpurea'
JUNE	plant	*B. thunbergii* 'Dart's Red Lady'
JULY	plant	
AUG	plant	*B. thunbergii* 'Aurea'
SEPT	plant	*B. thunbergii* 'Harlequin'
OCT	plant	Evergreen
NOV	plant	*B. candidula*
DEC	/	*B.* × *stenophylla*

BUTTERFLY BUSH

Buddleja davidii

Irresistible to butterflies that cluster on its nectar-rich flowers, varieties of Buddleja davidii *make summer special.*

Spectacular blooms, large handsome leaves and an ability to grow almost anywhere sunny, buddleja is a good choice for beginners.

FEATURES

There are three distinctive, hardy species: deciduous *Buddleja davidii*, whose cone-shaped flowers are dark purple, purplish red, pink, white or blue; *B. alternifolia*, yielding a waterfall of shoots sleeved with soft purple flowers; and evergreen *B. globosa*, with its clusters of small orange balls.

CONDITIONS

Aspect   These plants perform best in full sun, but tolerate slight shade; *B. davidii* resists chilly winds.

Site   Thriving in most soils, they prefer a well-drained position enriched with organic matter.

GROWING METHOD

Feeding   Boost growth by sprinkling bone meal around the shrub in April and October and hoeing it in. Take care not to damage roots. Water new plants regularly in spring and summer to encourage robust growth and bounteous blossom. Mulching helps to retain soil moisture in droughty spells.

Propagation   All kinds are easily increased from soft-tip cuttings in early summer and hardwood cuttings in autumn.

Problems   Control leaf-crippling aphids with pirimicarb, rotenone, permethrin or pyrethrins. *B. alternifolia*, grown as a standard, needs staking throughout its life.

PRUNING

B. davidii: Cut back the previous year's flowering shoots to within 5cm (2in) of the base in March.

B. alternifolia and globosa: Unlike *B. davidii*, which flowers on its current-year shoots, both *B. alternifolia* and *B. globosa* bloom on wood produced the previous year. Keep them youthful and flowering freely by shortening to the base a third of the oldest stems when the flowers fade.

BUTTERFLY BUSH AT A GLANCE

Hardy, deciduous and evergreen or semi-evergreen shrubs. Cones or globes of blossom light up summer. Hardy to -10°C (14°F).

		RECOMMENDED VARIETIES
JAN	/	
FEB	/	*B. alternifolia*
MAR	plant, prune	*B. davidii* 'Black Knight'
APR	plant	*B. davidii* 'Dartmoor'
MAY	plant	*B. davidii* 'Empire Blue'
JUNE	flower, plant	*B. davidii* 'Peace'
JULY	flower, plant	*B. davidii* 'Pink Delight'
AUG	flower, plant	*B. davidii* 'Santana'
SEPT	plant	*B. fallowiana* 'Alba'
OCT	plant	*B. globosa*
NOV	plant	*B. × weyeriana*
DEC	/	

BUTTERFLY BUSH VARIETIES

LEFT: Buddleja globosa, also known as the orange ball tree, bears a wealth of blossom on new shoots in June.

RIGHT: Deep purple Buddleja 'Black Knight' associates strikingly with ferny and silvery-leaved Artemisia 'Powis Castle'.

ABOVE: Plant 'Peace', a large white-flowered form of Buddleja davidii, to contrast with a deep green conifer.

BELOW: 'Pink Delight' is famed for its immense and long-lasting blooms, which complement large and greyish-green leaves.

ABOVE: Dramatic from spring to autumn, 'Harlequin's glowing red flowers tip elegant, wand-like shoots sleeved with cream or yellow-margined leaves.

ABOVE: 'Nanho Purple' is a small variety in all its parts and is good for narrow borders or small gardens.

BOX
Buxus

Drought-resisting common box makes a tight, neat plant in full sun. Tiny, yellow flowers stud shoots in spring.

Here, box clipped to create serpentine hedges focuses attention on the beauty of the brick paving, raised lily pond and garden bench.

FEATURES

Both common box (*Buxus sempervirens*), to around 4.5m (15ft), and lower-growing, small-leaved (Japanese) box (*B. microphylla japonica*) are favoured for planting in tubs and large pots and clipping into drumsticks, spirals, balls, pyramids and other forms of topiary. *B. sempervirens* 'Suffruticosa' makes the best low hedge. Box is long-lived and slow growing. If unclipped, it attains little more than 90cm (3ft) within 4–5 years. Common box has darker, more pointed foliage than the Japanese form, where leaves are shinier and lighter green. In spring, tiny, starry and delicately perfumed, yellowish-green flowers appear in leaf axils.

BOX AT A GLANCE

A hardy evergreen for topiary or low hedges. Variegated forms must be positioned in full sun. Hardy to -25°C (-13°F).

JAN	/	RECOMMENDED VARIETIES
FEB	/	
MAR	/	*B. microphylla* 'Winter Gem'
APR	flower, prune	*B. microphylla* 'Faulkner'
MAY	plant, prune	*B. sempervirens*
JUNE	flower, plant	*B. sempervirens* 'Handsworthensis'
JULY	plant, prune	
AUG	plant, prune	*B. sempervirens* 'Suffruticosa'
SEPT	plant	*B. sempervirens* 'Elegantissima'
OCT	/	
NOV	/	
DEC	/	

CONDITIONS

Aspect — Plants are more compact in full sun than shade, in which the foliage has less appeal. Creamy-mottled forms must be grown in good light or the variegation will fade to green.

Soil — Box thrives on chalk but also prospers on a wide range of other soils. Good drainage is vital. Enrich impoverished areas with bulky organic manure several weeks before planting.

GROWING METHOD

Feeding — Encourage lustrous leaves by fortifying planting holes with fish, blood and bone meal or Growmore, and topdressing the root area with bone meal in spring and autumn. These plants are not heavy feeders and normally flourish if you do forget to fertilise them. Established box tolerate fairly dry conditions.

Propagation — Box species can be grown from seed but varieties must be increased from semi-ripe cuttings from early to mid-autumn. Plants may also be divided in mid-spring.

Problems — If not fed regularly, box is rather slow to establish on poor, sandy soil.

PRUNING

After planting, use hedging shears to shorten shoots by a third to encourage a bushy habit. Trim hedges and topiary from April to August. If a bush is old and gaunt and needs revitalising, cut it hard back in April or May. Keep stumps moist to help them sprout. Cut out any all-green shoots on variegated plants.

BOTTLEBRUSH
Callistemon

Bottlebrush flowers are most commonly bright red but they can also be mauve, cream and gold. It is obvious how this evergreen shrub gained its name.

A handsome shrub, callistemon thrives in a sheltered, sunny spot.

FEATURES

Commonly called bottlebrush because its flower – principally stamens – reminds you of a bottle cleaner, the blooms enclasp slender stems clad with narrow, deep green leaves. There are several choice kinds. Hardiest is reckoned to be *Callistemon sieberi*, whose spikes of creamy-yellow flowers appear from late spring to summer. Also appealing are willow-leaved *C. salignus*, a species that glows with red, pink or mauve flowers; *C. rigidus*, another hardyish, red-flowered kind for 'borderline' gardens; and rich matt-red *C. linearis*, the narrow-leaved bottlebrush. Lemon-scented *C. citrinus* 'Splendens' treats us to a memorable display of soft, pinkish-red, new shoots and vivid crimson flowers. All grow to around 2.1m (7ft). Create a focus by underplanting a wall-trained shrub with white petunias.

BOTTLEBRUSH AT A GLANCE

An evergreen, frost-tender shrub with scarlet or creamy-yellow, bottlebrush flowers in June and July. Hardy to -5°C (23°F).

JAN	/	
FEB	/	
MAR	/	RECOMMENDED VARIETIES
APR	plant, prune	
MAY	plant	*C. citrinus* 'Splendens'
JUN	flower, plant	*C. linearis*
JULY	flower, prune	*C. rigidus*
AUG	plant	*C. salignus*
SEPT	plant	*C. sieberi*
OCT	/	
NOV	/	
DEC	/	

CONDITIONS

Aspect   Callistemon flowers best if fan-trained against a sheltered, sunny wall that is never shaded. This showy Australian is not for chilly gardens whipped by icy winds. If in doubt, consign it to a conservatory.

Soil   Preferring organically rich, light, loamy soil that drains freely, it thrives in clay if you add grit and bulky organics to improve aeration.

GROWING METHOD

Feeding   Callistemon copes reasonably well without added fertiliser but performs better if fed with fish, blood and bone meal in spring and midsummer.
Water new plantings regularly to encourage robust growth and rapid establishment. Mature plants tolerate long, dry periods but flower more profusely if the soil is moist.

Propagation   The species are easily grown from seed, but named varieties must be raised from semi-ripe cuttings, ideally with a heel of wood, in late summer.

Problems   Avoid alkaline soils in which leaves may turn pale yellow and die, and north- or east-facing sites, where cold winds may shrivel new shoots.

PRUNING

Trimming is not normally required, but occasional cutting back when blooms fade helps to keep growth compact and branches furnished with fresh green shoots.
Old shrubs can be rejuvenated if you prune them back quite hard in spring, but remove only a third of the bush in any one year. Keep stumps moist to encourage new growth.

CAMELLIA
Camellia

The exquisite beauty of delicately tinted camellia blooms – so effective in a vase – makes spring memorable.

Lime hating and thriving on deep, cool, leafy soil, flamboyant and long-flowering camellias associate stunningly with azaleas.

FEATURES

Glossy-leaved and showered with blossom, evergreen camellias are a great asset. Some species and varieties flower successively from late autumn through to spring. Blooms are white, pink, deep rose or crimson, and suffusions of these colours. Ranging in size from 1.2–4.5m (4–15ft), most varieties flower when 2–3 years old and mature within ten years. They grow to a great age. Plant them to form a statement in a lawn or mixed shrub border, or set them in a large pot or tub and clip them to form a loose obelisk, pyramid or drumstick. They also make a dashing flowering hedge.

CAMELLIA AT A GLANCE

Evergreen, frost-tender or hardy shrub with single, semi-double or fully double blooms. Hardiness according to species.

		RECOMMENDED VARIETIES
JAN	flower	
FEB	flower	*C. japonica* 'Adolphe Audusson'
MAR	flower	
APR	plant	*C. japonica* 'Berenice Boddy'
MAY	plant, prune	
JUNE	plant, prune	*C. reticulata* 'Captain Rawes'
JULY	plant	*C. sasanqua* 'Fuji-No-Mine'
AUG	plant	
SEPT	plant	*C. sasanqua* 'Nodami-Ushiro'
OCT	flower	
NOV	flower	*C.* x *williamsii* 'Donation'
DEC	flower	

Selection

Most camellias species come from China and Japan; some from N. India and the Himalayas. They have now been extensively hybridised to yield a wide range of varieties. Specialist camellia nurseries and garden centres display flowering plants in spring. Choose a variety suited to the position you have in mind.

Types

There are four main types of camellia.
Camellia japonica: Large and glossy leaved, hardier varieties will prosper in sheltered spots in the north of England and Scotland. Its varieties brighten autumn to spring.
C. sasanqua: Autumn-flowered, from October to December, it thrives outdoors in the south. From the Midlands northward, varieties are better planted in pots, displayed outdoors for summer and transferred to a cool conservatory, porch or greenhouse for flowering in autumn.
C. reticulata: Flowering from February to April, varieties can be grown outside in warm, sheltered, southern gardens. Elsewhere, display them under glass.
C. x *williamsii*: Producing tough, weather-resistant foliage, and flowering from November to April, its varieties bloom freely despite low light intensity. Each group is discussed in more detail on pages 20–21.

CONDITIONS

Aspect

Camellias in southern England grow best in sheltered, dappled shade. From the Midlands up to Scotland, set them in full sun or very light shade to ensure that blossom buds develop from July to October. Protect them

CAMELLIA

RIGHT: Dense, upright and slow growing, 'Wilamina' is a small, double, incurved variety of Camellia japonica. Blooms last well when cut and hold for a long time on the bush.

BELOW: Prized for its deep pink, outer petals that shade into a creamy-white centre, 'Buttons and Bows', sadly not available in Britain, is a medium-sized, formal, double hybrid of Camellia saluenensis. It flowers over a long period.

ABOVE: Vigorous and compact, Camellia japonica 'Nuccio's Gem' is a formal, double variety with spirally arranged petals. Just a whiff of frost can result in brown-speckled petals.

BELOW: 'Scentuous' is a small, informal, double hybrid of Camellia japonica 'Tiffany' and the species C. lutchuensis. Its creamy-white flowers have pale pink outer petals and the perfume of C. lutchuensis. It blooms profusely.

RIGHT: 'Wynne Rayner' is a saluenensis seedling. From early to mid-spring, a profusion of blooms is borne on freely branching stems clad with smallish, glossy green leaves

Camellia sasanqua

Sasanquas start the camellia season by producing flowers, depending on variety, from autumn to mid-winter. They make a wonderful show in a sheltered border or cool conservatory.

The smaller, more compact varieties, such as single, rose-pink 'Tanya' and double, bright rose-red 'Shishigashira', make good container plants.

Others worth a little cosseting are fast-growing 'Fuji-No-Mine', whose pure white, double blooms are borne on slender shoots; and bushy, upright 'Nodami-Ushiro', a sumptuous, semi-double, deep pink that pleases for weeks.

Camellia reticulata

This species presents us with the largest and most spectacular of all camellia blooms, but the shrubs themselves have a sparse, open-branching habit. Many of the more recently developed hybrids are crosses between *C. japonica* and *C. reticulata*. The result is a more leafy shrub that blooms longer with flowers that are more impressive.

To perform well, *C. reticulata* needs lighter, more free-draining soil than other camellias. Choice varieties are rose-pink 'Arbutus Gum' and carmine-rose 'Captain Rawes'.

Camellia japonica

This is the species that most people think of when camellias are mentioned. There is a wide range of varieties in white to pale or dark pink or red. There are picotee and bicolours. They are usually classified by flower type: that is, single, semi-double and formal double. There are also peony and anemone forms.

VARIETIES

BELOW: *'Betty Ridley', a rarely seen, sumptuous and profusely blooming, formal, double variety of* Camellia japonica, *is worth seeking from a specialist grower. Here it is compared with the tiny pink flower of the species,* C. rosiflora.

ABOVE: A rapturous but seldom seen white, flushed-pink and semi-double variety of Camellia vernalis, *'Star Upon Star' is usually grouped with* C. sasanqua *because of similarities in habit and uses. Blooming late in spring, it is an upright grower and ideal for small gardens and patio pots.*

BELOW: 'Desire', a large, formal, double variety of Camellia japonica, *bears arresting, mainly white petals, with rims delicately flushed with cerise pink.*

ABOVE: A collector's piece you may have to search for, 'Lois Shinault' is a large-flowered variety of Camellia reticulata, *whose semi-double, orchid-pink flowers of fluted petals display a showy boss of golden stamens.*

Some varieties produce sports – flowers of a different colour to the parent's. These 'sports' are a source of new varieties.

Varieties of *C. japonica* – they flower from late autumn to spring – may be grown in patio tubs or planted as border specimens. They also provide a fabulous backcloth to smaller shrubs and herbaceous perennials. Varieties include: White – 'Mary Costa': Unusual anemone form with incurving petals; upright growth. 'Lily Pons': Single to semi-double with long, narrow petals around a barrel of stamens.

Pink – 'Berenice Boddy': Semi-double; light pink with deeper pink under petals. Vigorous, spreading.
Red – 'Adolphe Audusson': Semi-double; good glossy leaves, open upright growth. 'C. M. Hovey': Formal double rose red; freely produced blooms.
Bicolour – 'Lavinia Maggi': Formal double; carmine-red and pink stripes on a white background.
Picotee – 'Margaret Davis' Informal double to loose peony; white petals rimmed with red; upright.

Camellia x williamsii

This is a very fine group of camellias bred by crossing *C. japonica* with *C. saluenensis*. The original crosses were made in Cornwall by J.C. Williams, who gave them their name. Available in the same colour range as other camellias, most are semi-double. Eagerly sought are: semi-double, orchid-pink 'Donation'; anemone-centred, creamy-white 'Jury's Yellow'; deep rose-pink 'Elegant Beauty', also with an anemone centre; and formal, vibrant, double, pink 'Water Lily'.

Some Camellia reticulata *varieties reward you with a breathtaking display of large, ruffled blooms from mid-winter to spring.*

Rare Camellia lutchuensis *treats you to a bounty of small and deliciously scented blooms from autumn to spring.*

Site

from hot, drying or frosty winds. Ideally, position plants where early morning sunlight does not heat up frosted blossom buds and cause frozen tissues to rupture. Sasanqua varieties tolerate more sun than most other camellias and reticulatas need full sun for part of the day. Some varieties of *Camellia japonica*, such as 'The Czar' and 'Emperor of Russia', happily take full sun. They need very acid, well-drained soil rich in decomposed organic matter. Heavy, badly drained soils cause root rot and plants often die. Fortify thin, sandy soils with well-rotted leaf mould or bulky manure, before planting.

GROWING METHOD

Feeding

Encourage lustrous leaves and a wealth of blossom by applying a balanced ericaceous fertiliser in April and July. It is vital that border soil or container compost is always moist, so water daily, if necessary, during prolonged hot spells. Mulch with crumbly, bulky organic manure to conserve moisture, but keep it well away from the stem, lest it causes bark to rot.

Propagation

Increase plants from semi-ripe cuttings in late summer, removing a thin strip of bark from the base to reveal wood and stimulate rooting. Leaf-bud cuttings, 2.5cm (1in) or so long, again 'wounding' the base of the shoot, are also taken then. Alternatively, layer low, flexible shoots from mid-spring to late summer. Some varieties, which are very hard to grow from cuttings, are grafted on to understocks of *C. sasanqua*.

Problems

You may encounter the following:
*Bud drop: This can be caused by overwet or overdry soils, root rot or root disturbance. Some very late-flowering varieties may have buds literally pushed off the stem by new spring growth.
*Brown petals and balled blooms: This usually

occurs when buds or flowers are lit by early morning sunshine while still wet with dew. Petals may be scorched and some buds 'ball' and fail to open. Some varieties with clusters of big buds are prone to this. Gently breaking off some of the buds when they first form helps to reduce balling.
*Oedema: If plants are overwet and conditions overcast, small, brown, corky swellings may develop on leaves. Reduce watering and try to improve air circulation.
*Scale insects: These may be found on the upper or lower leaf surface. Limpet-like scales suck sap and debilitate plants. Spraying with malathion controls them, but spray only in cool or cloudy weather so that it does not scorch leaves.
*Leaf gall: This causes abnormal thickening and discoloration of new growth. It occurs in spring and is caused by a fungus. Pick off and destroy affected leaves before spores disperse.
*Viruses: May be responsible for variable, bright yellow patterns on leaves, or ring spot. Rings develop on leaves. As the leaf ages it becomes yellowish; the centre of the ring becomes bright green. There is no cure for viruses, but plants rarely lose much vigour or have their blooming affected. Pick off the worst-looking leaves if they are spoiling your plant's appearance.

PRUNING

Little pruning is needed. Cutting blooms for the vase is usually enough to keep plants compact. However, any thin, spindly, unproductive growth should be removed from the centre of the shrub after flowering. Ageing, overgrown camellias can be rejuvenated by quite heavy pruning, provided cuts are made directly above a leaf bud. If severe pruning is necessary, do it in stages, over two years, to avoid stressing the plant.

CALIFORNIAN LILAC
Ceanothus

Evergreen ceanothus, such as 'Puget Blue', are best fan-trained against a warm wall.

There are few more riveting, spring- and early summer-flowering shrubs – ideal for light soils that dry out quickly – than evergreen members of the Californian lilac family.

FEATURES

Prized for their massed clusters of principally pale blue to deep violet-blue, powderpuff blooms, there are evergreen and deciduous varieties. They range from carpeters to imposing bushes of around 4.5m (15ft) high. Most evergreens, such as 'Blue Mound' and *Ceanothus thyrsiflorus* 'Edinensis', bloom from May to June. Two exceptions, 'Autumnal Blue' and 'Burkwoodii', perform from July to September. The best of the deciduous group – pink 'Marie Simon' and blue 'Gloire de Versailles' – flower from July to October.

CALIFORNIAN LILAC AT A GLANCE

Evergreen or deciduous shrubs with blue or pink blooms from spring to early autumn. Hardy to -10°C (14°F).

JAN	/	
FEB	/	RECOMMENDED VARIETIES
MAR	plant, prune	Evergreen
APR	plant, prune	'Blue Mound'
MAY	flower, plant	'Cascade'
JUN	flower, plant	'Concha'
JULY	flower, plant	'Puget Blue'
AUG	flower, plant	*C. thyrsiflorus* 'Repens'
SEPT	flower, plant	'Zanzibar' (variegated)
OCT	flower, plant	Deciduous
NOV	/	'Gloire de Versailles'
DEC	/	'Marie Simon'
		'Perle Rose'

CONDITIONS

Aspect All kinds, especially evergreen varieties which are best grown against a south-facing wall, need a sunny, sheltered spot where air circulates freely.

Site Ceanothus prospers on well-drained clay loam, sandy or humus-rich, gravelly soils. It will not thrive on heavy clay that waterlogs in winter, where roots are liable to rot.

GROWING METHOD

Feeding Keep plants lustrous and flowering freely by applying bone meal in spring and autumn. Breaking down slowly, it is rich in phosphates, which encourage robust root growth.
In its native habitat, this plant receives rain only in winter and has adapted to very dry summers.

Propagation Most varieties are grown from semi-ripe cuttings taken from mid- to late summer.

Problems Ceanothus is susceptible to root rot, caused by wet soil. It is seldom troubled by pests.

PRUNING

Evergreen varieties: Trim spring-flowering kinds when blooms fade in early summer, and cut late summer performers in April.

Deciduous varieties: In early spring, shorten the previous year's flowered shoots to within 5–7.5cm (2–3in) of the older wood.

CALIFORNIAN LILAC VARIETIES

ABOVE: 'Concha' forms a dense, arching, evergreen bush to 1.5m (5ft) high and 1.8m (6ft) across and enriches spring with a profusion of red-budded, deep blue flowers. Find it a warm, sunny spot and it will handsomely reward you.

ABOVE: A sumptuous, evergreen variety, 'Dark Star' is prized for its spicy perfumed, purplish-blue blossoms borne in showy bunches on shoot tips in late spring. Small, oval, toothed leaves clad an umbrella of branches.

ABOVE: Glorifying May and June, Ceanothus dentatus floribundus, as its name implies, is so massed with terminal or lateral clusters of glowing ultramarine-blue flowers that its small, evergreen leaves tend to 'disappear'.

ABOVE: From mid- to late spring, the rounded to oval, deeply veined, evergreen leaves of Santa Barbara ceanothus (Ceanothus impressus) complement a dashing display of clustered, dark blue flowers on shoot tips.

BELOW: A robust form of evergreen Ceanothus arboreus soaring to 6m (20ft), 'Trewithen Blue' drips with scented, mid-blue flowers in late spring and early summer. Plant it to make a spectacular focal point for a large, sunny, sheltered lawn.

BELOW: Plant evergreen 'Puget Blue', a zestful variety of Ceanothus impressus, to clothe a sunny wall or fence. In spring, every shoot is thickly sleeved with rich indigo-blue flowers. Never prune it hard, for older growth seldom regenerates.

JAPONICA
Chaenomeles

Eye-catching when grown as an espalier against a north- or east-facing wall, chaenomeles yields clusters of bloom from late winter to late spring.

Midwinter splendour: flowering quince is sleeved with blossom when many shrubs are resting.

FEATURES

Also known as japonica or flowering quince, this spiny, deciduous shrub makes a colourful bush to 2.1m (7ft) high or, if espalier-trained against a wall or fence, a striking drape to 2.7m (9ft). Long-lived, it flowers early in life and reaches maturity in 3–5 years. It is valued for its thickly clustered blooms that transform bare branches from mid-winter to early spring. Flowers are followed by small, fragrant, quince-like fruits that ripen to bright yellow. Fruits are edible and make delicious jams and preserves. Showy varieties include apricot 'Geisha Girl', pink 'Moerloesii', white 'Nivalis' and large, bright crimson 'Rowallane'. In borders, it makes a showy, rounded background plant for smaller shrubs, perennials, bulbs and annuals.

JAPONICA AT A GLANCE

A hardy deciduous shrub, its clusters of white, pink or red, saucer-shaped flowers brighten spring. Hardy to -25°C (-13°F).

JAN	/	
FEB	/	
MAR	flower, plant	**RECOMMENDED VARIETIES**
APR	flower, prune	For walls
MAY	flower, prune	'Geisha Girl'
JUNE	plant	'Moerloesii'
JULY	prune	'Nivalis'
AUG	plant	'Simonii'
SEPT	plant	For bushes
OCT	plant	'Lemon and Lime'
NOV	plant	'Pink Lady'
DEC	/	'Knaphill Scarlet'
		'Rowallane'

CONDITIONS

Aspect Usefully adaptable, chaenomeles thrives in full sun or light shade, does not mind chilly winds and colours cold, north- or east-facing walls.

Site Though it prefers well-drained soil, it tolerates heavy, waterlogged clay. Help sandy soils stay cool and moist by working in plenty of bulky manure or well-rotted garden compost.

GROWING METHOD

Feeding Unlike many other shrubs, chaenomeles thrives in poorish soil. For best results, build fertility by topdressing the root area with pelleted chicken manure, fish, blood or bone meal or Growmore in spring and midsummer. Water plants regularly in their first year.

Propagation Take semi-ripe cuttings in late summer or detach and replant rooted suckers in autumn.

Problems If coral spot appears – shoots are pimpled with coral-pink or orange pustules – cut back to healthy, white wood and burn prunings. Paint stumps with fungicidal pruning compound.

PRUNING

Bushes: Apart from removing crowded shoots when flowers fade in spring, no regular cutting back is required.

Wall trained: Young plants: Tie espaliered shoots to a wire frame. In July, cut back to five leaves shoots growing away from the wall. Reduce to two buds further growth from shortened shoots. Established plants: Shorten the previous year's side shoots to two or three leaves when flowers fade in spring.

MEXICAN ORANGE BLOSSOM
Choisya ternata

Wafting citrus scent on a warm breeze, starry-flowered, evergreen Mexican orange blooms in spring and autumn.

Harmonising beautifully with a pink-flowering Japanese cherry, Mexican orange blossom performs best in a sheltered, sunny spot.

FEATURES

A spring prince, evergreen *Choisya ternata*, to 1.8m (6ft) or more high, is regaled with orange-fragrant, starry, white flowers in April and May and again in October. Its glossy, trefoil leaves spill citrus scent when you brush against them.

'Sundance', a smaller, golden-leaved form, is particularly striking in winter when its foliage assumes orange-yellow tints. Intriguingly different – leaves are long and narrow – 'Aztec Pearl' bears pink-budded, white blossoms.

CHOISYA AT A GLANCE

Hardy evergreen shrubs – 'Sundance' has yellow leaves – with orange-scented, white flowers in spring. Hardy to -10ºC (14ºF).

JAN	/	
FEB	/	
MAR	/	
APR	flower, plant	RECOMMENDED VARIETIES
MAY	flower, prune	*C. ternata*
JUNE	flower, prune	*C. ternata* 'Sundance'
JULY	plant	*C. ternata* 'Aztec Pearl'
AUG	plant	
SEPT	flower, plant	
OCT	/	
NOV	/	
DEC	/	

CONDITIONS

Aspect Full sun or light shade, but 'Sundance' needs more light than *C. ternata* or 'Aztec Pearl', otherwise its leaves will pale to green and lose their appeal. In northern gardens, position all three kinds against a warm, sunny wall.

Site Choisya thrives in fertile, acid, neutral or alkaline soil. Enrich nutrient-starved, quick-draining, sandy loam or stony patches with bulky organic manure.

GROWING METHOD

Feeding Apply a complete plant food, such as Growmore or fish, blood and bone meal in early spring and midsummer. Water regularly and copiously in long, dry periods.

Propagation Increase choisya from semi-ripe cuttings from mid- to late summer, or layer stems from early to late summer.

Problems No specific pests or diseases but flowering diminishes if shrubs are not pruned regularly and left to become woody.

PRUNING

In chilly areas, cut back frost-damaged shoots to healthy, white wood in spring. Keep mature bushes – over five years old – flowering freely by removing from the base a third of the older branches when blooms fade in May or June.

ROCK ROSE
Cistus

A rapid succession of crumpled, silky, often-blotched blooms in white, pink and cerise are your reward for planting cistus.

A Mediterranean drought resister, free-flowering rock roses are also coveted for their aromatic leaves, which distil 'honey' on a warm day.

FEATURES

A dandyish Mediterranean native, evergreen cistus delights us from June to August with a daily succession of saucer-shaped, crumpled, silky blooms. Bushes range in size from carpeting, white and maroon-blotched *Cistus lusitanicus* 'Decumbens', to 60cm (2ft) high, to white and yellow-centred *C. laurifolius*, an imposing sentinel that rises to 1.5m (5ft). There are pink-, crimson- and lilac-flowered varieties, too. All varieties perform early in life and taller kinds make stunning, informal flowering hedges. Small, pot or tub-grown species and varieties, such as neat and bushy 'Silver Pink' with its greyish-silvery leaves, illuminate a sun-baked patio.

ROCK ROSE AT A GLANCE

Drought-resisting evergreen for light soil, it is smothered with white, pink or red blooms in summer. Hardy to -5°C (23°F).

JAN	/	
FEB	/	**RECOMMENDED VARIETIES**
MAR	/	
		Small – up to 90cm (3ft)
APR	plant, prune	*C. x corbariensis*
		'Silver Pink'
MAY	flower, plant	*C. x skanbergii*
JUNE	flower, plant	'Sunset'
JULY	flower, plant	Tall – over 90cm (3ft)
AUG	plant, prune	'Alan Fradd'
		C. laurifolius
SEPT	plant	*C. x purpureus*
OCT	/	
NOV	/	
DEC	/	

CONDITIONS

Aspect   Rock roses must have full sun all day to make compact, free-flowering plants. They do not mind exposed sites or salt-laden breezes, but may be damaged by frosty winds. Avoid growing them in areas of high rainfall as blooms are spoilt by prolonged, wet weather.

Site   Plants make the strongest growth on humus-rich, sandy or gravelly loam, which drains quickly; they are less spirited on heavy, badly drained soils. In nature, rock roses flourish on porous limestone. If your soil is acid, boost growth by adding lime before planting.

GROWING METHOD

Feeding   These plants need little or no fertiliser. Apply a light dressing of bone meal in spring and autumn.
Once plants are growing strongly, water is seldom needed, even during weeks of drought.

Propagation   Take semi-ripe cuttings in summer. Species can be grown from seeds or cuttings. Varieties must be raised from cuttings.

Problems   No particular pest or disease afflicts cistus, but hard pruning into older wood can inhibit stumps from re-growing.

PRUNING

Encourage newly planted shrubs to branch freely and make dense bushes by pinching out shoot tips several times throughout the first two summers. Cut back frost-damaged stems to healthy growth in spring.

SHRUBBY BINDWEED
Convolvulus cneorum

Canopied with dazzling white blossom from June to August, Convolvulus cneorum*, with red campion, flourishes in full sun.*

No garden? Plant silky-leaved, shrubby convolvulus to emblazon a patio pot or tub with a massed display of funnel-shaped flowers.

FEATURES

A coveted, silvery, silky-leaved evergreen whose pink buds open to flared, white and yellow-eyed, trumpet blooms from June to August, *Convolvulus cneorum* makes a low hummock to 45cm (18in) high and 75cm (2.5ft) across and has many uses.

Create a feature all will admire by associating it with *Ceanothus* 'Zanzibar', prized for its powder-blue flowers and golden-variegated leaves.

Plant shrubby bindweed to highlight a rock garden or star in a patio pot or deep windowbox.

It is not fully hardy, so consign it to a very sheltered border and cover it in late autumn with several layers of bubble plastic draped over an open-topped wigwam of canes. Make sure the plastic does not touch its foliage. If you plant it in a patio pot for summer, move it to a cold greenhouse for winter.

CONDITIONS

Aspect   Find it a sheltered, sunny spot – it revels against a south- or west-facing wall – where it will not be damaged by chilly winds.

Site   Not fussy, it thrives in well-drained, acid to neutral soil. If your garden has badly drained clay, work in plenty of grit or sharp sand or set the plant on a raised bed. It is vital that roots are not 'treading' water.

GROWING METHOD

Feeding   Boost growth by working fish, blood and bone meal or Growmore into the root area in April and July. Add a slow-release fertiliser to patio tub compost. If planting coincides with a droughty spell, foliar feed weekly to help the plant absorb nutrients more quickly.
Water copiously after planting to settle soil around the roots. Follow by mulching with a 5cm (2 in) layer of well-rotted organic material to conserve moisture.

Propagation   Increase shrubby bindweed from semi-ripe 'heeled' cuttings of new side shoots from late summer to early autumn.

Problems   If hard frost causes shoot tips to die back, prune them to just above a healthy bud in late spring.

PRUNING

Pruning is unnecessary unless the plant is ageing. Then, in early spring, reduce gaunt and woody stems by half their length, cutting to just above a joint or to new shoots. Keep stumps moist to help them sprout. The best way to do this, apart from sprinkling them with water, is to coat them with a plastic-based anti-transpirant, normally used for helping Christmas trees retain their needles.

SHRUBBY BINDWEED AT A GLANCE

A borderline hardy evergreen with soft, silvery leaves; trumpet-shaped flowers appear from June to August. Hardy to -10°C (14°F).

		RECOMMENDED VARIETIES
JAN	shield from frost	
FEB	shield from frost	(only the species
MAR	/	*C. cneorum* is grown)
APR	plant, prune	
MAY	plant	
JUNE	flower, plant	
JULY	flower, plant	
AUG	plant	
SEPT	plant	
OCT	/	
NOV	/	
DEC	/	

FLOWERING DOGWOOD
Cornus

In mid-spring, white or pink-tinted flowers (bracts) transform the Pacific dogwood (Cornus nuttallii) into a fascinating talking point.

Late winter sees the bare branches of Cornelian cherry (Cornus mas) studded with a multitude of tiny, primrose-yellow blossoms.

FEATURES

Suddenly, in late winter – from February to March – sulphur-yellow, powderpuff blooms light up bare, slender stems. *Cornus mas* has few rivals.

In spring, when flowers fade, oval, pointed, vivid green leaves unfold. Small, edible, cherry-shaped, red fruits, good for jam, form in autumn when leaves assume reddish-purple tints before falling.

A coveted, leaf-shedding native of Europe and Western Asia, it slowly forms a handsome globe to around 4.5m (15ft) high and across. It can also be planted to create a stocky, dense flowering hedge.

Dramatically different, the Pacific dogwood (*C. nuttalli*) bears a plethora of saucer-shaped white, pink-tinged bracts (flowers), which light up late spring. When its flowers fade, they are fetchingly replaced by orbs of multi-seeded fruits.

FLOWERING DOGWOOD AT A GLANCE

Cornus mas has sulphur-yellow flowers in February; *C. nuttallii* bears whitish-pink blooms in June. Hardy to -15°C (4°F).

JAN	/	RECOMMENDED VARIETIES
FEB	flower	*C. mas* 'Aurea'
MAR	flower, prune	*C. mas*
APR	plant	'Aureoelegantissima'
MAY	flower, plant	*C. mas* 'Hillier's Upright'
JUNE	flower, plant	*C. mas* 'Variegata'
JULY	plant	*C. nuttallii* 'Colrigo
AUG	plant	Giant'
SEPT	plant	
OCT	plant	
NOV	plant	
DEC	/	

CONDITIONS

Aspect Though performing better in full sun, both species are good contenders for lightly shaded spots. In deep shade, they form a looser, less symmetrical branching system. They are not harmed by cold winds.

Site *C. mas* thrives on virtually any soil, from light sand to heavy clay and chalk, provided it is not waterlogged. *C nuttallii* needs acid, fertile conditions. Enrich impoverished sand and chalk with bulky organic manure or well-rotted garden compost.

GROWING METHOD

Propagation *C. mas:* Take semi-ripe cuttings of maturing side shoots – ready when the bark at the base of the stem turns brown and firms up – in late summer.
C. nuttalli: Best increased from soft-tip cuttings from early to midsummer.

Feeding Boost growth by topdressing the root area with a granular form of complete plant food, or fish, blood and bone meal in spring and midsummer. Water in if the soil is dry.
In droughty spells, keep shoots vigorous by soaking the root area or digging a moat around the shrub and repeatedly filling it with water. Follow by mulching thickly with moisture-retaining, well-rotted garden compost, bark or cocoa shell.

Problems *C. mas* and *C. nuttallii* have a rugged constitution and are seldom troubled by pests and diseases.

PRUNING

Pruning is not needed, apart from removing awkwardly placed shoots after flowering. Use sharp secateurs and cut to just above a shoot.

SMOKE BUSH
Cotinus coggygria

In early summer, Cotinus *'Notcutt's Variety' treats us to a fabulous display of amber, pink and purple 'smoke-like' inflorescences.*

Prized for its richly hued leaves, Cotinus *'Royal Purple' contrasts fetchingly with green-leaved berberis.*

FEATURES

Remarkably drought-resistant shrub, *Cotinus coggygria*, from central and southern Europe, is appealing twice a year: in June and July when its plumy, 15–20cm (6–8in) flowers are reminiscent of pink smoke; and in autumn when leaves are suffused with vibrant, fiery or sunset hues.

Growing slowly to form an obelisk 2.7m (9ft) by 1.8m (6ft), purple-leaved varieties associate beautifully with lemon-yellow-leaved mock orange (*Philadelphus coronarius* 'Aureus'). Purple-leaved kinds also make a fetching host for scrambling *Lathyrus grandiflorus*, an exuberant, pink-flowered perennial pea.

If you do not have sufficient border space for a smoke bush, set it in a large tub of tree and shrub compost and position it to form a statement on your patio or at the end of a path. Plant a pair of shrubs to frame the entrance to a wide driveway.

SMOKE BUSH AT A GLANCE

Green or purple leaves assume sunset autumn tints. 'Smoky' flowering plumes make summer special. Hardy to -15°C (4°F).

JAN	/	RECOMMENDED VARIETIES
FEB	/	
MAR	plant, prune	'Atropurpurea'
APR	plant, prune	'Grace'
MAY	plant	'Notcutt's Variety'
JUNE	flower, plant	'Royal Purple'
JULY	flower, plant	
AUG	plant	
SEPT	plant	
OCT	plant	
NOV	plant	
DEC	/	

CONDITIONS

Aspect Stalwarts both, green- and purple-leaved varieties are very hardy and unaffected by cold winds.

Site The green-leaved family excels in full sun or light shade, but purple-liveried varieties must have bright sunshine or their foliage will pale to insipid green. All prefer humus-rich soil enriched with bulky organic manure or well-rotted garden compost, but they will survive without stress on thin, sandy loam.

GROWING METHODS

Feeding Fortify the root area with fish, blood and bone meal, or Growmore, twice a year: in spring and midsummer. Water it in if the soil is dry.

Propagation Increase plants from semi-ripe cuttings of new shoots from mid- to late summer. Root them in a lightly shaded garden frame or on a brightly lit windowsill.

Problems If shoot tips die after a very hard winter, shorten them to live buds in early spring. Should mildew attack purple-leaved varieties, control it by spraying with fungicide containing carbendazim.

PRUNING

Choose one of three methods:
For a mass of flowers on a large shrub, prune only to remove dead wood.
To achieve a balance of foliage and flowers, take out a third of the oldest shoots each spring.
For dashing foliage, spectacular autumn colour and no flowers – ideal for purple-leaved varieties – cut back all shoots to 15cm (6in) from the base in early spring. Keep cuts moist to encourage regrowth.

COTONEASTER

Cotoneaster

Herringbone cotoneaster (Cotoneaster horizontalis) *is splendid for covering walls. Pinkish-white flowers are followed by scarlet berries.*

Cotoneaster conspicuus 'Decorus's froth of white summer blossom preludes a feast of bright red autumn fruits.

FEATURES

This versatile, evergreen, semi-evergreen or deciduous family ranges in height from carpeters of 30cm (12in) to towering bushes more than 3m (10ft) high.

Choice kinds are dense and weed-suppressing, evergreen 'Coral Beauty', whose glowing orange berries light up autumn; semi-evergreen *Cotoneaster horizontalis*, ideal for clothing a bank or wall beneath a ground floor window; and semi-evergreen 'Cornubia', an imposing, arching bush to 3m (10ft).

Evergreen *C. lacteus* and semi-evergreen *C. simonsii* make splendid, low, flowering and berrying hedges.

Sprays of small, white spring flowers are followed by a glowing autumn to winter display of red or yellow fruits. Cotoneasters take 5–10 years to mature, depending on species and conditions, and are long-lived. Fruits are nutritious food for garden birds and winter migrants.

COTONEASTER AT A GLANCE

Deciduous, semi- or fully evergreen shrub; white blossom heralds an autumn display of vibrant fruits. Hardy to -25°C (-13°F).

JAN	/	RECOMMENDED VARIETIES
FEB	/	
MAR	plant	Ground covering to 30cm (12in)
APR	plant	'Coral Beauty'
MAY	flower, prune	'Oakwood'
JUNE	flower	'Skogholm'
JULY	plant	Small bushes (30–80cm/ 12–32in)
AUG	plant	
SEPT	plant	*C. conspicuus* 'Decorus'
		C. horizontalis
OCT	plant, prune	Taller kinds
NOV	plant, prune	'Cornubia'
DEC	/	

CONDITIONS

Aspect All kinds grow best and flower and fruit more freely in full sun. They will tolerate partial shade, but shoots are looser and berries sparse.

Site Cotoneasters prefer well-drained, medium to heavyish loam, but any reasonably fertile soil encourages stocky growth. Improve thin, sandy or gravelly areas by digging in bulky, humus-forming, well-rotted manure, decayed garden compost or leaf mould.

GROWING METHOD

Feeding Not essential, but an application of Growmore or fish, blood and bone meal, carefully pricked into the root area in spring and midsummer, encourages lustrous leaves.

If you are growing a small-leafed, bushy variety such as *C. simonsii* as a close-planted hedge, apply fertiliser in spring and summer. Water newly planted cotoneasters regularly in spring and summer to help them grow away quickly. Once established, they will tolerate long periods without supplementary watering.

Propagation Take semi-ripe cuttings from mid- to late summer; layer shoots from spring to summer.

Problems Fireblight: Causing flowers to wilt and wither – they appear scorched – it is controlled by cutting back affected shoots to healthy, white wood. Burn prunings. If you live in Northern Ireland, Isle of Man or the Channel Islands, you must notify your local branch of Ministry of Agriculture, Fisheries and Food.

PRUNING

Keep plants flowering and fruiting well by removing one stem in three. Tackle evergreens in mid-spring and deciduous kinds in mid-autumn.

HAWTHORN
Crataegus

Hawthorn's abundant, milky-scented, white flowers in early summer are followed by clusters of scarlet or orange berries in autumn and winter.

A traditional English hedgerow shrub, hawthorn (Crataegus monogyna) *also makes an elegant, small flowering tree.*

FEATURES

Architectural, deciduous hawthorns – ideal for focal points or screening – can be shrubby or grow into small trees to 4.5m (15ft). Clad with lobed or toothed leaves, suffused with fiery scarlet tints in autumn, blossom mantles shoots in May and June. Bright orange or red berries – birds adore them – persist into winter. Stems are usually spiny and native may or quickthorn (*Crataegus monogyna*) makes a formidable barrier. Others, such as glossy-leaved *C. x lavallei*, whose large clusters of white blossom are followed by orange berries coupled with richly autumn-hued leaves, and deep red-flowered *C. laevigata* 'Paul's Scarlet, make fetching sentinels.

HAWTHORN AT A GLANCE

Large, deciduous bushes or small trees, their summer blossom is followed by orange or scarlet fruits. Hardy to -25°C (-13°F).

JAN	/	
FEB	prune	RECOMMENDED VARIETIES
MAR	plant	'Crimson Cloud'
APR	plant	*C. x grignonensis*
MAY	flower, plant	*C. x lavallei*
JUNE	flower	'Paul's Scarlet'
JULY	prune	'Rosea Flore Pleno'
AUG	prune	
SEPT	/	
OCT	plant	
NOV	plant, prune	
DEC	prune	

CONDITIONS

Aspect Stalwarts for exposed upland gardens raked by wind, or those fringing the sea, where leaves are powdered with salt, hawthorn flowers best in full sun. In light shade, bushes have a more open habit and fewer blooms.

Site Though hawthorn prefers deep and heavyish but well-drained soils, it will tolerate light, sandy or gravelly ground. Improve thin soils by working in plenty of bulky organic matter.

GROWING METHOD

Feeding Work bone meal into the soil in spring and autumn to ensure a continuous supply of root-promoting phosphates.
Water copiously in the first year after planting. Thereafter, when hawthorn is established, it is seldom stressed by drought.

Propagation Raise species from seed, from berries mixed with damp sand and placed in a flower pot. Break dormancy by positioning the pot in the coldest part of the garden. In spring, remove seeds and sow them in an outdoor seed bed. Seedlings quickly appear.

Problems Powdery mildew can whiten leaves. Control it by spraying with carbendazim, mancozeb or triforine with bupirimate.

PRUNING

Bushes: Encourage a profusion of blossom by shortening the previous year's shoots by two-thirds in late winter.

Hedges: Clip in mid-July and in winter.

BROOM
Cytisus

From May to June, Cytisus scoparius *illuminates a sunny border with golden-yellow blossom. Contrast it with a purple-leaved cotinus.*

Bearing cone-shaped, richly pineapple-scented blooms in early summer, Cytisus battandieri *is best fan-trained against a sunny wall.*

FEATURES

Treating us to whippy stemmed and thickly clustered cascades of fragrant, pea flowers, deciduous and butter-yellow-flowered *Cytisus scoparius* and its kaleidoscope-hued hybrids make May and June special.

Plant them singly to punctuate a border, or group several of one colour or in harmonising shades to create an unforgettable statement. Its fetching, leaf-shedding relation Moroccan (pineapple) broom (*C. battandieri*) is famed for its June display of pineapple-scented cones of bright yellow blooms amid silvery, tri-lobed leaves. It has a lax, floppy habit so train it to embrace a sunny wall or frame a patio door. Alternatively, plant it to entwine a tall, metal obelisk in a border or at the end of a path.

When in flower, a warm, breezy day wafts crushed pineapple scent around the garden.

BROOM AT A GLANCE

Massed, tiny, pea blooms or chunky, golden flower cones brighten borders from late spring to early summer. Hardy to -10°C (14°F).

		RECOMMENDED VARIETIES
JAN	/	
FEB	/	*C. battandieri*
MAR	plant	*C. scoparius* 'Andreanus'
APR	plant	*C. scoparius* 'Burkwoodii'
MAY	flower, plant	*C. scoparius* 'Goldfinch'
JUNE	flower, prune	*C. scoparius* 'Killeney Red'
JULY	plant	
AUG	plant	*C. scoparius* 'Killeney Salmon'
SEPT	plant	
OCT	plant	*C. scoparius* 'Lena'
NOV	/	*C. scoparius* 'Zeelandia'
DEC	/	

CONDITIONS

Aspect   *C. scoparius* and its varieties are hardier than *C. battandieri*, which needs to be sheltered from chilly winds. Both flower at their best in full sun.

Site   Encourage robust growth by setting plants in free-draining and well-manured, neutral or acid, sandy soil. Lime tends to cause weak, pale green leaves.

Feeding   After adding balanced fertiliser to planting holes, encourage sturdy growth by topdressing the root area with fish, blood and bone meal in spring and again in midsummer. If your soil is chalky and hybrids are suffering from iron deficiency, help them recover by applying a soil-acidifying fertiliser.

Propagation   Increase *C. scoparius* and *C. battandieri* from semi-ripe cuttings taken from mid- to late summer.

Problems   When *C. scoparius* and its hybrids become woody and flower less – after ten or so years – they cannot be refurbished by hard pruning, so it is best to replace them with young, potted plants.

Occasionally, in summer, leaf buds develop into cauliflower-like growths covered with silvery hairs. Gall mites cause them. There is no chemical control, so remove affected plants and replace them with healthy stock.

PRUNING

Keep *C. scoparius* and its hybrids youthful and ablaze with flowers in spring by shearing flowered stems to just above older growth when pods form. *C. battandieri* isn't normally pruned, but cut out badly placed and weak stems after flowering If you are growing it against a wall, tie in new shoots then.

DAPHNE
Daphne

Sweetly scented Daphne odora 'Aureomarginata' *rewards us with clusters of pinkish-white flowers in late winter.*

Lime-tolerant daphnes – this is Daphne odora *– have an unfounded reputation for being difficult. Find them a cool, moist and sunny spot.*

FEATURES

Grown primarily for their sweetly fragrant blooms, daphnes are best planted close to a living room where, on a warm day with a window open, scent wafts indoors. Alternatively, set bushes in pots or tubs beside a garden seat. Herald spring with deciduous *Daphne mezereum*, to 90cm (3ft), with upright stems sleeved with starry, purplish-red flowers. Slightly taller but spreading and evergreen *D. odora* 'Aureomarginata', with its cream-edged, green leaves that complement clusters of pinkish-white blooms, also flowers then. Later, from May to June, evergreen *D. burkwoodii* 'Somerset', wondrous when filling a large pedestal urn and forming a focal point, exudes vanilla perfume from pale pink blooms.

DAPHNE AT A GLANCE

Deciduous or evergreen shrubs with purple-red to pink flowers from late winter to early summer. Hardy to -7°C (19°F).

		RECOMMENDED VARIETIES
JAN	/	
FEB	flower	*D. bholua*
MAR	flower, plant	*D. burkwoodii* 'Somerset'
APR	flower, plant	*D. cneorum*
MAY	flower, prune	*D. mezereum*
JUNE	flower, prune	*D. odora* 'Aureomarginata'
JULY	plant	*D. retusa*
AUG	plant	
SEPT	plant	
OCT	plant	
NOV	plant	
DEC	/	

CONDITIONS

Aspect Daphne prospers in full sun or very light shade. Shelter it from strong, drying winds.

Site It must have perfectly drained soil with a high organic content. Keep roots cool by mulching plants with well-decayed manure.

GROWING METHOD

Feeding Sustain strong flowering shoots by feeding with bone meal in spring and autumn. Encourage newly planted shrubs by liquid feeding with a high-potash fertiliser at weekly intervals from spring to summer.
Deep, regular watering is necessary for young plants in long, dry spells. Make sure the soil does not become soggy, for roots may rot.

Propagation Multiply plants by layering shoots from mid-spring to late summer or by taking semi-ripe cuttings from mid- to late summer.

Problems Sudden death is usually caused by root rot triggered by bad drainage. Daphne may also be attacked by blackening, leaf-spot fungi that speckle foliage. Control leaf spot by spraying with carbendazim or mancozeb. Viruses are also liable to attack daphne. Characterised by twisted and puckered leaves, there is no control, so dig up and burn affected plants.

PRUNING

No regular cutting back needed, apart from shortening young, straggly stems in spring to keep bushes tidy. Do not prune into older, black-barked wood, for stumps may not regenerate.

DEUTZIA
Deutzia

Flowering from spring to early summer, single, white-flowered Deutzia gracilis *makes a charming background to these late yellow primroses.*

Soaring to around 2.1m (7ft), Deutzia scabra *flaunts sprays of double, white or pink-tinged blooms from July to August.*

FEATURES

Profusely blooming, deciduous, upright or rounded deutzias are easy to grow and best displayed in a mixed border. All, apart from late-flowering *Deutzia monbeigii* with its small leaves, appealingly white beneath and complementing dense clusters of starry, white flowers from July to August, perform from May to July. An elegant, upright shrub, deutzia varies in height from deep carmine-pink-flowered *D.* x *rosea*, 80cm (32in) by 60cm (24in), to *D. scabra* 'Pride of Rochester', a handsome leviathan that soars to 2.1m (7ft). From June to July, its double, white blooms smother pleasingly, peeling-barked branches.

CONDITIONS

Aspect Deutzia prefers full sun but will tolerate light shade. Plants should be sheltered from strong, northerly or easterly winds.

Site This shrub flourishes on most well-drained soils, especially if fortified with organic matter.

GROWING METHOD

Feeding Undemanding, deutzia does not need regular feeding. If growth is poor, topdress the root area with Growmore or fish, blood and bone meal in spring and summer.

Propagation Multiply deutzia from hardwood cuttings from mid-autumn to early winter.

Problems Late spring frosts may damage blossom buds of May-flowering varieties, so position plants carefully if you garden in a frost pocket.

PRUNING

Encourage a wealth of blossom by cutting back to near ground level a third of the older branches when flowers fade. If stems bearing flower buds are killed by frost, shorten them to healthy wood.

DEUTZIA AT A GLANCE

Deciduous shrub with shoots clothed in single or double, pink or white blooms in spring and summer. Hardy to -25°C (-13°F).

JAN	/	**RECOMMENDED VARIETIES**
FEB	/	*D.* x *elegantissima*
MAR	plant	'Rosealind'
APR	plant	*D.* x *hybrida* 'Magician'
MAY	flower, plant	'Montrose'
JUNE	flower	*D. monbeigii*
JULY	flower, prune	*D.* x *rosea* 'Campanulata'
AUG	plant, prune	*D. scabra* 'Pride of
SEPT	plant	Rochester'
OCT	plant	
NOV	plant	
DEC	plant	

PRIDE OF MADEIRA
Echium candicans (fastuosum)

Tower of jewels is another evocative name for Echium candicans, *a remarkable, Canary Islands native.*

In a sheltered, frost-free garden, this amazing shrub will spread to 1.8m (6ft) across. Elsewhere, it should be grown in a container and overwintered under glass.

FEATURES

A somewhat sprawling shrub with grey-green leaves, Pride of Madeira is an exciting challenge. Growing to about 1.5m (5ft) high and spreading to 2.1m (7ft) or more, it produces long, fat spikes of sapphire to violet-blue flowers in late spring and early summer. Being frost tender, it is best grown in a pot and consigned to a high conservatory or large greenhouse. Move it to a sheltered, sunny patio or terrace in June and bring it indoors when nights turn chilly in September. It matures in 3–5 years and flowers early in life.

PRIDE OF MADEIRA AT A GLANCE

Frost tender, with blue flowers in summer. In chilly areas, it must be overwintered under glass. Hardy to -1°C (30°F).

JAN	shield from frost	RECOMMENDED VARIETIES
FEB	shield from frost	
MAR	shield from frost	*E. candicans*
APR	plant	
MAY	plant	
JUNE	flower, plant	
JULY	flower, prune	
AUG	flower, prune	
SEPT	flower, plant	
OCT	/	
NOV	/	
DEC	/	

CONDITIONS

Aspect   Echium needs full sun all day. Under glass, air must freely circulate.

Site   Set this plant in a large pot of multipurpose compost augmented with a quarter part Perlite to ensure good drainage. Pot it on in early spring when roots fill the container and mat the compost as the need for watering increases.

GROWING METHOD

Feeding   Boost growth by liquid feeding with a high-potash fertiliser, weekly from spring to late summer. Alternatively, insert aggregates of slow-release fertiliser granules into the compost in spring.

Watering: Echium tolerates very dry conditions and needs only an occasional soaking in prolonged droughty weather.

Propagation   Echium is raised from seed in spring or early summer. Alternatively, take semi-ripe heeled cuttings tugged from older stems, in midsummer. Root cuttings in a propagator heated to around 21°C (70°F).

Problems   No particular pest or disease troubles this plant. If aphids colonise shoot tips, tackle them with pirimicarb or natural pyrethrins.

PRUNING

Remove spent flower heads and shorten shoots outgrowing their allotted space.

HEATH
Erica

Plant a selection of lime-hating Erica cinerea *varieties and enjoy a succession of blossom from June to November.*

Performing from November to May, Erica carnea, *here complementing a golden-flowered berberis, is prized for its white, pink, red, lavender or mauve display.*

FEATURES

A large, vibrant-flowered group of bushy and carpeting, evergreen shrubs, 22.5cm–1.5m (9in–5ft) high, their thickly clustered, tubular or bell-shaped blooms in white and a confection of pink, purple, coral and crimson hues illuminate the year. Colour winter with varieties of *Erica* x *darleyensis* and *E. carnea*; cheer spring by grouping *E. arborea* and *E. erigena*; glorify summer and autumn with *E. cinerea*, *E. tetralix* and *E. vagans*.

Use them to brighten borders and rock gardens and suppress weeds. Ideally, associate them with dwarf conifers.

Create a tapestry of blossom by combining ericas with closely related varieties of ling (*Calluna vulgaris*), which flower from July to November, and Irish heath (*Daboecia cantabrica*). Some callunas, such as 'Beoley Gold', yield radiant golden foliage.

CONDITIONS

Aspect Most are very hardy, tolerate chilly winds and are ideal for exposed, upland gardens. Heathers must have full sun and good air circulation. Do not crowd plants.

Site While all varieties prefer acid soil, winter-flowering *Erica carnea* tolerates slightly alkaline conditions. Good drainage is vital. Mulch plants annually, in spring, with leaf mould or well-rotted garden compost.

GROWING METHOD

Feeding Established plants need little or no fertiliser. If the soil is very poor, fortify the root area with a balanced, acidifying fertiliser in spring.

Propagation Take semi-ripe heeled cuttings from early to late summer; layer shoots in mid-spring.

Problems Heathers quickly succumb to root rot in heavy or overwet soils.

PRUNING

Lightly shear flowered shoots when blooms fade. Never cut back into older wood. Tackle autumn- and winter-flowering varieties when new shoots appear in spring.

HEATH AT A GLANCE

Carpeting evergreens whose succession of blossom or foliage enchants us every month of the year. Hardy to -15°C (4°F).

		RECOMMENDED VARIETIES
JAN	flower	
FEB	flower	Spring flowering
MAR	flower	'Albert's Gold'
APR	plant, prune	'Viking'
MAY	flower, plant	Summer flowering
JUNE	flower, prune	'C.D. Eason'
JULY	flower, prune	'Pink Ice'
AUG	flower, plant	Autumn flowering
SEPT	flower, plant	'Andrew Proudley'
OCT	flower	'Stefanie'
NOV	flower	Winter flowering
DEC	flower	'Ann Sparkes'

HEATH VARIETIES

ABOVE: A fetching variety of ling, Calluna 'Kerstin', makes a dense mound to 30cm (12in) high and across and treats us to a profusion of single, mauve flowers from August to September. In full sun, its shoot tips are bright yellow – a bonus in winter.

RIGHT: A newish, golden-leaved hybrid to around 1.2m (4ft), Erica 'Valerie Griffiths' makes a glowing, year-round focal point for a heather garden. Alternatively, it can be planted in a large pot to decorate a patio or terrace. Pale pink flowers appear from August to October.

ABOVE: Also called Irish or Mediterranean heath, Erica erigena has honey-scented sprays of deep lilac-pink flowers in spring, thickly borne on 2.4m (8ft) stems. An imposing sentinel, it can be planted to form a good, dense hedge which is trimmed when flowers fade.

BELOW: Colourful throughout the seasons, Calluna 'Red Carpet', just 15cm (6in) high, is a good choice for small gardens. Studded with spires of mauve blossom from August to September, its leaves, golden in summer, assume orange-red tints in winter.

ABOVE: There are few more wondrous heathery sights than a mature bush of Erica x veitchii 'Gold Tips'. Massed cones of white blossom appear from March to June and new spring foliage is tipped with gold.

LEFT: A golden-leaved beacon to 25cm (10in) high, lime-tolerant Erica x darleyensis 'Mary Helen' unfolds a wealth of single, pink flowers from February to April. Group it in full sunshine where its leaves will not lose their radiance, or plant it to colour a deep windowbox.

ESCALLONIA
Escallonia

A prized and colourful shrub, especially for windy gardens, Escallonia 'Pride of Donard' rewards us with sprays of pink blossom.

Semi-evergreen and summer-blossoming escallonia can be trained to form a fetching, flowering hedge in mild districts.

FEATURES

Escallonia is evergreen in mild districts but semi-evergreen elsewhere. Its arching shoots, festooned with sprays of clustered, tubular, white, pink or red flowers amid small, glossy leaves, highlight the summer months. Long-lived, it makes a stunning sentinel to around 1.8m (6ft) and as a flowering hedge. The hardiest species – ideal for windswept, seaside gardens – *Escallonia rubra macrantha* delights us with many rose-crimson flowers. Other choice kinds are rich pink 'Donard Radiance', rose-pink 'Donard Star' and golden-leaved and rosy-red-flowered 'Gold Brian'.

ESCALLONIA AT A GLANCE

Evergreen or semi-evergreen, its arching shoots are sleeved with white, pink or red flowers in summer. Hardy to -10°C (14°F).

JAN	/	
FEB	/	RECOMMENDED VARIETIES
MAR	/	'Donard Radiance'
APR	plant, prune	'Donard Seedling'
MAY	plant, prune	'Glory of Donard'
JUNE	flower, plant	'Gold Brian'
JULY	flower, plant	'Iveyi'
AUG	flower, plant	*E. rubra macrantha*
SEPT	flower, plant	'Slieve Donard'
OCT	/	
NOV	/	
DEC	/	

CONDITIONS

Aspect   Though escallonia needs full sun to flower best, it does not object to light shade. Most hybrids tolerate buffeting wind. In chilly or northern gardens, it should be planted against a sheltered, south-facing wall.

Site   This splendid shrub thrives in any well-drained soil. Aerate heavy clay by working in grit or gravel; fortify light and nutrient-starved, sandy soils by working in plenty of bulky, moisture-conserving organic materials.

GROWING METHOD

Feeding   Ensure a steady release of plant foods by applying bone meal in spring and autumn. After planting, water freely and regularly in dry spells to encourage strong new growth. Keep roots cool and questing freely by mulching with shredded bark, cocoa shell, crumbly manure or rotted garden compost.

Propagation   Multiply choice varieties from semi-ripe cuttings from the middle of summer to the middle of autumn.

Problems   Cut darkly stained shoots infected with silver leaf back to healthy, white wood 15cm (6in) beyond the point of infection.

PRUNING

Shorten a third of the oldest stems to near ground level when blooms fade. In cold gardens, cut back frost-damaged growth to strong, new shoots in late spring.

SPURGE
Euphorbia species

The showiest part of a euphorbia 'flower' is a pair of lime-green bracts (modified leaves). The true flower is a small, yellow 'button'.

Perfect for tempering hot orange and yellow flowers, Euphorbia characias wulfenii *performs best in full sun.*

FEATURES

Pleasing us with a spring to early summer display of yellowish-green, bottlebrush blooms on stems clad with whorls of evergreen leaves, *Euphorbia characias wulfenii* is architecturally magnificent. Forming a dense bush to 1.2m (4ft), it is ideal for interplanting and tempering vibrant orange, yellow and red-flowered border perennials. This euphorbia lives for around ten or more years and matures within 2–3 years. Use it in a shrub border or as a background for annuals and perennials. A related sculptural gem, for sheltered gardens only, is Madeiran honey spurge (*E. mellifera*).

Seducing us with large and exotic, lance-shaped leaves, its honey-scented, brownish flower clusters form on shoot tips in spring.

CONDITIONS

Aspect   Hardy *E. characias* needs full sun; more tender *E. mellifera* requires a sheltered spot.

Site   These sub-shrubs thrive almost anywhere, even in heavy soils, provided drainage is good. Boost growth in light, sandy soil by incorporating bulky organic manure.

GROWING METHOD

Feeding   Feeding is not essential but apply fish, blood and bone meal, Growmore or pelleted chicken manure in spring.

Propagation   Take soft-tip cuttings from mid-spring to early summer.

Problems   When crowded, euphorbia may become infected with grey mould, a disease that coats leaves and stems with furry, brownish-grey mould. Control it by cutting infected shoots back to healthy tissue and spraying with carbendazim.

PRUNING

Wear gloves and safety glasses to cut back flowered stems to ground level in early summer. Strong, new shoots replace them and bloom the following year.

SPURGE AT A GLANCE

Evergreen shrub, *E. characias wulfenii* produces huge, bottlebrush blooms from spring to early summer. Hardy to -12°C (10°F).

		RECOMMENDED VARIETIES
JAN	/	
FEB	/	*E. characias* 'John Tomlinson'
MAR	/	
APR	flower, plant	*E. characias* 'Lambrook Gold'
MAY	flower, plant	
JUNE	flower, prune	*E. characias* 'Margery Fish Group'
JULY	prune, plant	
AUG	plant	*E. characias* 'Purple and Gold'
SEPT	plant	
OCT	/	*E. characias wulfenii*
NOV	/	*E. mellifera*
DEC	/	

SPURGE VARIETIES

RIGHT: Ideal for carpeting shady spots and improvished areas beneath trees, Euphorbia amygdaloides robbiae *rarely needs watering. From April to June, it delights us with lime-green columns of blossom. Even when faded, they retain their charm.*

ABOVE: Enchanting when draping a hot, sunny, rock-garden outcrop or spilling from a drystone retaining wall, drought-resisting and semi-prostrate *Euphorbia myrsinites is easy to grow. In spring, terminal clusters of bright greenish-yellow blooms top shoots clothed with spiralling, blue-grey leaves.*

RIGHT: Bearing distinctive, greenish, bottlebrush blooms from early spring to early summer, *Euphorbia characias wulfenii is sculpturally appealing. Plant it to form a focal point in a wide border or flank a path or drive.*

BELOW: No euphorbia collection is complete without *Euphorbia polychroma, a closely related herbaceous species. In spring, its captivating dome of glowing sulphur-yellow flowers lights up a border. The brighter the site the more intensely hued blooms are.*

LEFT: There are few more dramatic sights in spring than a bed of *Euphorbia amygdaloides 'Purpurea', whose young, reddish-purple leaves contrast with heads of acid-yellow flowers. Group it with small, white daffodils.*

FIG-LEAVED PALM
Fatsia japonica

Exotic-fingered leaves are your reward for growing evergreen Fatsia japonica. *Plant it in a tub to light up a shady patio or terrace.*

Delighting us with its large heads of creamy, bobble-like blooms in autumn, when most other shrubs are resting, fatsia tolerates dry soil.

FEATURES

Stunningly architectural, the large, glossy, palmate leaves of *Fatsia japonica* have an appealing leathery texture. In autumn, it delights us with an exotic candelabrum of golf-ball-sized, white flower heads. Each comprises many tiny, five-petalled flowers. Large, handsome, black berries follow them. A native of South Korea and Japan, it has a spreading, suckering habit and makes a dome to 1.8m (6ft) high and 2.4m (8ft) across. Plant it to enhance a large patio tub. It tolerates air pollution, so is a good shrub for towns or cities. It resists salty sea breezes, too. Dramatise a sunny border by grouping it with golden-leaved yuccas.

If you plant fatsia in a border, create a striking feature by embracing it with tussock-forming and ground-covering *Liriope muscari*, whose spikes of bell-shaped, violet flowers complement the fatsia's white bobbles.

FIG-LEAVED PALM AT A GLANCE

Dashing focal point for a lightly shaded spot. Intriguing bobbles of white blossom appear in autumn. Hardy to -10°C (4°F).

		RECOMMENDED VARIETIES
JAN	/	
FEB	/	'Variegata'
MAR	/	
APR	prune, plant	
MAY	plant	
JUNE	plant	
JULY	plant	
AUG	plant	
SEPT	plant, flower	
OCT	flower	
NOV	flower	
DEC	/	

CONDITIONS

Aspect Ideal for brightening sheltered and lightly shaded spots, it objects to hot sunshine, which may scorch its leaves. Protect from icy winds, which also brown its foliage.

Site It is not fussy about soil but prefers deep rich loam, which encourages the largest, most sculpturally appealing leaves. Add grit or gravel to soggy clay to improve drainage. Apply an acidifying fertiliser, such as sequestered iron, to chalky soil to reduce risk of chlorosis. When iron is 'locked up' by calcium, roots cannot absorb it and leaves turn yellow and die.

GROWING METHOD

Feeding Boost lustrous foliage by topdressing the root area in spring, and again in summer, with fish, blood and bone meal, which enriches the soil's humus content and encourages beneficial micro-organisms. Alternatively, use quick-acting but short-lived Growmore to accelerate shoot development.

Water freely after planting to settle soil around roots. Follow with a 5cm (2in) mulch of old manure, bark or cocoa shell.

Propagation Take semi-ripe cuttings in summer and strike them in a closed cold frame or on a sunny windowsill.

Problems Control aphids, which colonise and cripple shoot tips, by spraying with a systemic insecticide.

PRUNING

Apart from maintaining its symmetry by shortening long branches or frost-damaged shoots in spring, cutting to a joint or lower shoot, no regular attention is necessary.

GOLDEN BELL BUSH
Forsythia

Forming a bushy shrub to around 1.8m (6ft), generous flowering and sun-loving Forsythia 'Lynwood' is draped with blossom in spring.

Create a vibrant March marriage of yellow blossom and scarlet bark by associating forsythia with a coppiced clumps of Cornus alba 'Sibirica'.

FEATURES

Heartening indeed is the spring sight of a bush thickly laden with starry, sulphur-yellow or deep golden blooms. Flowers open naturally from March to April. Enjoy an earlier show by cutting fat-budded stems in February and forcing them into bloom in a warm room. There are two principal kinds: border forsythia (*Forsythia x intermedia*), which makes a rounded shrub to 2.4m (8ft) high and across, and *F. suspensa*, a snaking, weeping or trailing form, enchanting when cascading over a wall or over the lower branches of pink, weeping cherry. Border forsythia can be also grown as a flowering hedge or trained to frame a window or doorway. Neat and compact 'Golden Curls', just 60cm (2ft) high and 90cm (3ft) across, is ideal for a small garden.

GOLDEN BELL BUSH AT A GLANCE

Deciduous, bush and trailing/weeping varieties have flowers clothing year-old shoots in spring. Hardy to -25°C (-13°F).

		RECOMMENDED VARIETIES
JAN	/	
FEB	/	'Fiesta'
MAR	flower, plant	'Gold Cluster'
APR	flower, plant	'Golden Curls'
MAY	plant, prune	'Gold Tide'
JUNE	plant	'Lynwood'
JULY	plant	'Spring Glory'
AUG	plant	'Suspensa'
SEPT	plant	'Weekend'
OCT	plant	
NOV	plant	
DEC	plant	

CONDITIONS

Aspect A sunny position is vital. In shade a multitude of shoots form but many will refuse to flower. Growth also becomes loose and weak. Forsythia braves cold wind.

Site This plant grows strongly in most well-drained soils, from heavy clay to light sand and chalk. Fortify impoverished borders, especially where roots from nearby trees invade, with humus-forming, old, crumbly or proprietary composted manure, well-rotted garden compost, shredded bark or leaf mould.

GROWING METHOD

Feeding If the soil was initially enriched with plant foods, forsythia seldom needs further feeding. If growth is slow, boost it by topdressing with a balanced granular fertiliser. Alternatively, liquid feed weekly with a high-nitrogen fertiliser from spring to midsummer.
Water newly planted shrubs copiously and frequently to help them recover quickly.

Propagation Layer low flexible shoots from spring to late summer or take hardwood cuttings in autumn.

Problems Occasionally – the cause is not known – warty galls distort stems. Overcome them by cutting back affected shoots to healthy wood and burning them.

PRUNING

Once established, keep plants youthful and flowering freely by removing from the base a third of the oldest shoots when flowers fade. Clip hedges at the same time of year, so that flower buds form for the following year.

GENISTA
Genista

Swagged with golden flowers in midsummer, the Mount Etna broom makes a striking shrubby tree and revels in a warm, dry spot.

Here Genista lydia, *a hummock of blossom in June, looks good with silvery-leaved and yellow-flowered* Brachyglottis 'Sunshine'.

FEATURES

Small or rushy leaved and wiry stemmed, this accommodating deciduous family, related to broom, embraces showy, prostrate carpeters and small or large bushes to several metres high. All sport pea-like flowers in various shades of yellow.

From May to June, cushion-like Spanish gorse (*Genista hispanica*), hummocky and cascading *G. lydia* and dazzling, carpeting *G. pilosa* 'Vancouver Gold' treat us to a display so radiant that it deceives you into thinking it is sunny when it is not.

Come July and August, the spring brigade is eclipsed by bushy *G. tinctoria* 'Royal Gold' and the imposing and fragrant Mount Etna broom (*G. aetnensis*), with its pendulous, rush-like shoots that shower from branches 2.7m (9ft) high.

CONDITIONS

Aspect Hardy and tolerating exposed positions, all genistas perform best in full sun. Drought resisting, they are ideal for hot spots that cannot easily be watered.

Site Happiest in humus-rich and light, free-draining sand and loam, they also prosper in clay if you work in gravel and crumbly organic materials to improve drainage.
Usefully, *G. tinctoria* excels in chalky soil.

GROWING METHOD

Feeding Encourage robust growth by topdressing the root area with a slow-release organic fertiliser, such as bone meal, in spring and autumn.

Water freely in droughty periods and keep roots cool and active by mulching with old manure, well-rotted garden compost or bark.

Propagation Increase genista from semi-ripe cuttings of side shoots from mid- to late summer. Root them in pots on a bright windowsill or in a lightly shaded cold frame.

Problems Normally trouble free.

PRUNING

Avoid cutting back *G. aetnensis*, *G. lydia* and *G. tinctoria*, whose stumps may not regrow. You can, however, rejuvenate ageing *G. hispanica* by shortening old woody stems by two-thirds their length in spring. Keep large stumps moist in dry, windy weather to help them regenerate.

GENISTA AT A GLANCE

Deciduous spring- or summer-flowering bushes, they need full sunshine to flower bounteously. Hardy to -10ºC (14ºF).

Month	Activity		RECOMMENDED VARIETIES
JAN	/		
FEB	/		*G. aetnensis*
MAR	plant		*G. hispanica*
APR	plant, prune		*G. pilosa* 'Vancouver Gold'
MAY	flower, prune		*G. tinctoria* 'Flore Pleno'
JUNE	flower, plant		*G. tinctoria* 'Royal Gold'
JULY	flower, plant		
AUG	flower, plant		
SEPT	plant		
OCT	plant		
NOV	plant		
DEC	/		

WITCH HAZEL
Hamamelis

A heartening winter vision is spidery, sulphur-yellow-flowered
Hamamelis x intermedia *'Pallida' underplanted with snowdrops.*

A bonus of orange, scarlet and red autumn tints prelude Hamamelis
vernalis *'Sandra's late winter display of cadmium-yellow 'spiders'.*

FEATURES

Shining like a beacon on a winter's day, witch hazel's twisted, spidery perfumed flowers thickly clothe bare, spreading branches. Hardy and bushy, 2.4–3m (8–10ft) high and across, this deciduous shrub is a slow but worthwhile grower that rewards patience. Ideally, set it in a lawn with snowdrops and daffodils.

Choice kinds among several undemanding species and varieties are large, golden-flowered Chinese witch hazel (*Hamamelis mollis*), which blooms from December to March. *H.* x *intermedia* is a hybrid that flowers from February to March and has given us upright and primrose-hued 'Westerstede', sulphur-yellow 'Pallida', orange and yellow 'Diane' and coppery orange 'Jelena'.

The large, soft-hairy leaves of *H. mollis* turn butter-yellow in autumn. The foliage of 'Diane' and 'Jelena' is suffused with orange-red before falling. Equally fascinating is the less fragrant Japanese witch hazel (*H. japonica* 'Zuccariniana'), which from January to March produces a multitude of pale lemon 'spiders'.

CONDITIONS

Aspect   Hamamelis flowers more freely in full sun and makes a shapelier, more compact bush than in light shade, in which branches are thinner and further apart and leaves larger. Position coppery red-flowered varieties where the sun shines at an angle through their petals and renders them fetchingly translucent.

Site   Preferring well-drained, fertile, neutral to acid soil, hamamelis dislikes alkaline, chalky conditions, which causes leaves to become chlorotic. Enrich sandy soils with old manure.

GROWING METHOD

Feeding   Water freely after planting to encourage rapid recovery. Each spring, mulch with crumbly manure, bark or well-rotted garden compost to keep roots cool and active. In April, topdress the root area with fish, blood and bone meal or Growmore, repeating in July.

Propagation   Layer shoots from mid-spring to late summer. Alternatively, take soft-tip cuttings in late spring and root them in a mist propagating unit in a temperature of 21°C (70°F).

Problems   When buying plants, opt for those more than four years old, which, unlike younger ones, have a greater chance of succeeding.

PRUNING

Not necessary, but if badly placed stems need removing or shortening, to improve symmetry, use sharp secateurs or loppers when flowers fade, in early spring.

WITCH HAZEL AT A GLANCE

Deciduous and forming a chalice of spreading branches, yellow or orange blooms sleeve stems in winter. Hardy to -25°C (-13°F).

JAN	flower	RECOMMENDED VARIETIES
FEB	flower	*H. japonica* 'Zuccariniana'
MAR	plant, prune	*H.* x *intermedia* 'Diane'
APR	plant	*H.* x *intermedia* 'Jelena'
MAY	plant	*H.* x *intermedia* 'Pallida'
JUN	plant	*H.* x *intermedia* 'Westerstede'
JULY	plant	*H. mollis*
AUG	plant	
SEPT	plant	
OCT	plant	
NOV	plant	
DEC	flower	

SHRUBBY VERONICA
Hebe

Salt-spray resistant, hebes are ideal for brightening coastal gardens in mild districts. They also tolerate air pollution.

Hebe 'Great Orme', here contrasting effectively with an upright cypress, is studded with shapely spikes of blossom from July to October.

FEATURES

An immense and handsome family of small, rounded-leaved or larger, willow-leaved, evergreen New Zealanders, hebes' clustered or cone-shaped spikes of massed, tiny flowers illuminate May to late October. Resisting air pollution, these shrubs are ideal for seaside gardens in mild districts. There are three main, easy and reliable groups:

Carpeters: Forming a dense mat of weed-suppressing foliage to around 30cm (12in) high, choice kinds include silvery grey-leaved and white-flowered *Hebe pinguifolia* 'Pagei'.

Bushes: Making bushy globes to 1.2m (4ft), stunning varieties are 'Autumn Glory', whose violet-blue blossoms colour June to November, and 'Great Orme', smothered with bright pink flowers from July to October.

Taller kinds : Imposing sentinels to 1.8–3m (6–10ft), lilac-white *H. salicifolia* is a prince among them.

CONDITIONS

Aspect   Hebes need an open position in full sun to make robust and free-flowering growth.

Site   Most well-drained soils suit these plants, but they perform best in humus-rich, sandy loam.

GROWING METHOD

Feeding   Boost growth by sprinkling fish, blood and bone meal, Growmore or pelleted chicken manure over the root area in April and July. Water copiously to establish new plants. Once growing strongly, little water is needed.

Propagation   Take soft-tip cuttings in early summer and semi-ripe cuttings in midsummer.

Problems   Control leaf spot disease by spraying with carbendazim or mancozeb.

PRUNING

Cut back late-flowering varieties to within 6in of the base, every two years in spring, to encourage bounteous blossom. Remove any reverted, green-leaved stems from variegated varieties as soon as they appear.

SHRUBBY VERONICA AT A GLANCE

Evergreen carpeters or bushes clothed with clustered, cone-shaped flowers in white and many other colours. Hardy to -5°C (23°F).

		RECOMMENDED VARIETIES
JAN	/	
FEB	/	'Carl Teschner'
MAR	/	*H. x franciscana* 'Blue Gem'
APR	plant, prune	'Great Orme'
MAY	flower, prune	*H. hulkeana*
JUNE	flower, plant	'Midsummer Beauty'
JULY	flower, plant	*H. pinguifolia* 'Pagei'
AUG	flower, plant	*H. speciosa* 'Gauntlettii'
SEPT	flower, plant	'Wiri Charm'
OCT	flower	
NOV	/	
DEC	/	

SUN ROSE
Helianthemum

Deep red and yellow-eyed blooms and silvery leaves make 'Supreme' a prized variety.

Enjoy a tapestry of blossom by growing sun roses to cascade from a retaining wall. Here plants are camouflaging gaunt, leggy, rose stems.

FEATURES

Varieties of evergreen *Helianthemem nummularium*, commonly called rock or sun rose, make a spreading 10–30cm (4–12in) mound to 90cm (36in) across. From May to July, a network of wiry stems clothed with small, oval leaves are almost hidden beneath a daily succession of single or double flowers in glowing shades of yellow, pink, red, orange, white or terracotta. Flowers tend to close up on dull days. Sun roses are perfect for draping rock garden pockets, cascading from retaining walls and aproning roses and other bushes flanking a path. They are not long-lived but easily raised from cuttings of maturing, current-year shoots.

CONDITIONS

Aspect Sun rose performs best in an open, brightly lit and airy position where it has room to spread and is not crowded by other plants. Avoid even a hint of shade in which growth is looser, less comely and flowering is inhibited.

Site This shrub needs well-drained and slightly alkaline conditions. Add garden lime to raise the pH of acid soil.

GROWING METHOD

Feeding Boost lustrous foliage and a wealth of blossom by applying a high-potash rose fertiliser in spring and the middle of summer.
Water newly planted shrubs regularly and copiously to help them recover quickly and make good root growth in their first year. Thereafter, they will need watering only in droughty weather. Mulch plants generously with spent mushroom compost.

Propagation Take semi-ripe heeled cuttings in midsummer. These should make flowering-sized plants by the following spring.

Problems Poor drainage or overwatering may kill plants. Powdery mildew can be a problem in crowded borders where air circulates sluggishly. Control this disease by thinning growth and spraying with carbendazim or bupirimate with triforine.

PRUNING

From early to midsummer, when blooms fade, shear back shoots to two-thirds their length. This not only keeps bushes trim and flowering well in spring, but often results in a second, smaller, flush of blossom in autumn.

SUN ROSE AT A GLANCE

A carpeting evergreen so thickly clothed with flowers from May to July that leaves are concealed by them. Hardy to -10°C (14°F).

		RECOMMENDED VARIETIES
JAN	/	
FEB	/	'Golden Queen'
MAR	/	'Henfield Brilliant'
APR	plant	'Raspberry Ripple'
MAY	flower, plant	'Red Orient'
JUN	flower, plant	'Supreme'
JULY	flower, plant	'The Bride'
AUG	plant, prune	'Wisley Pink'
SEPT	plant	'Wisley Primrose'
OCT	/	
NOV	/	
DEC	/	

HELIOTROPE
Heliotropium

Old-fashioned heliotrope or cherry pie is festooned with spicy-perfumed blooms from early summer until autumn, when chilly nights halt the display.

'Marine' is captivating if planted to cascade its deep violet flowers from a patio or terrace tub.

FEATURES

Heliotropium arborescens, also known as cherry pie, is a half-hardy, soft-stemmed, evergreen Peruvian shrub. Growing to 1.2m (4ft) high and across, it is usually bedded out for summer and overwintered in a frost-free greenhouse. A succession of vanilla-fragrant, mauve to purple flowers are borne from summer to the middle of autumn, or even longer under glass.
Plant it to spill from a border and on to paving, waterfall from a raised bed or beautify a patio tub. 'Lord Roberts', with very dark purple-green leaves and deep violet flowers, is probably the most popular variety.

HELIOTROPIUM AT A GLANCE

Frost-sensitive evergreen with richly fragrant, pink, purple, violet or white flowers, bedded out for summer. Hardy to 4°C (40°F).

JAN	/	
FEB	/	RECOMMENDED VARIETIES
MAR	/	'Dame Alice de Hales'
APR	plant, prune	'Chatsworth'
MAY	plant, prune	'Lord Roberts'
JUNE	flower, plant	'White Lady'
JULY	flower	'Netherhall White'
AUG	flower	'Princess Marina'
SEPT	flower	
OCT	flower	
NOV	flower	
DEC	/	

CONDITIONS

Aspect
Outdoors: Heliotrope needs a warm position sheltered from chilly winds. It flowers best in full sunshine.
Under glass: Provide full sun but reduce risk of leaf scorch by shading plants when the temperature rises above 24°C (75°F).

Site
Outdoors: The soil should be crumbly and well drained. Enrich thin, sandy patches with humus-forming, well-decayed manure.

GROWING METHOD

Feeding
Outdoors and under glass: Liquid feed weekly with a high-potash fertiliser from spring to late summer.
In late summer or early autumn, lift and pot up plants bedded out in borders and patio tub plants. Move them to a frost-free greenhouse or conservatory and keep the compost dry until late winter or early spring.

Propagation
Heliotrope is easily increased from soft-tip cuttings taken in spring, and semi-ripe cuttings struck in late summer.

Problems
Being half-hardy, this shrub must not be moved outdoors until frosts have finished in late May or early June.

PRUNING

Encourage new flowering stems by shortening a third of older, woody branches by half their length in early spring.

HIBISCUS
Hibiscus

A late-summer bonus of exotic, single or double, saucer-shaped blooms are your reward for growing a hardy hibiscus.

Healthy and seldom attracting pests and diseases, hibiscus is best planted in a sunny position so shoots ripen and flower well.

FEATURES

Also known as shrubby mallow, this deciduous, late summer statement is festooned with saucer-shaped blooms from July to September. Flowers are single or double and range in colour from white, pink and blue to purple. Several are bicoloured. Most popular varieties are violet-blue and white-eyed 'Blue Bird', white and crimson-eyed 'Hamabo' and rose-pink and dark-centred 'Woodbridge'. Long-lived, it makes an upright bush to 2.4m (8ft) high and across and flowers early in its life. It is very hardy.

CONDITIONS

Aspect   Hibiscus grows best and flowers prolifically in full sun. Shield it from icy winds. Avoid even light shade, for shoots will not ripen well and so flowering is impaired.

Site   This shrub thrives on well-drained, fertile, sandy loam but tolerates poorer soils. Enjoy good results by enriching the planting area with plenty of well-rotted organic matter.

GROWING METHOD

Feeding   Apply all-purpose plant food, such as fish, blood and bone meal or Growmore, in spring and again in midsummer.
Water regularly in spring and summer to help newly planted hibiscus recover quickly.

Propagation   Layer whippy shoots from mid-spring to late summer, and take semi-ripe heeled cuttings from late summer to early autumn.

Problems   Control aphids with pirimicarb, horticultural soap or natural pyrethrins.

PRUNING

Rejuvenate ageing shrubs by shortening them to half their height in spring. This is also the best time to cut back frost-damaged shoots.

HIBISCUS AT A GLANCE

Deciduous and slow growing, large, saucer-shaped, pink, blue or white blooms appear in late summer. Hardy to -15°C (4°F).

		RECOMMENDED VARIETIES
JAN	/	
FEB	/	'Blue Bird'
MAR	plant	'Bredon Springs'
APR	plant, prune	'Hamabo'
MAY	plant	'Lady Stanley'
JUNE	plant	'Lenny'
JULY	flower, plant	'Meehanii'
AUG	flower, plant	'Woodbridge'
SEPT	flower, plant	'William R. Smith'
OCT	plant	
NOV	plant	
DEC	/	

HYDRANGEA
Hydrangea

Ever popular hydrangea is a native of China and Japan. Ensure pink blossom by adding lime to the soil in spring. For ultramarine-blue flowers, feed with aluminium sulphate.

Position mophead and other hydrangeas in a sheltered spot in dappled shade.

FEATURES

Brightly studded with large, globular, mushroom-headed or broadly conical flowers, hydrangeas richly colour borders from July to September. Blooms come in white and shades of pink, blue or red. Long-lived, this deciduous shrub grows 50cm–2.4m (20in–8ft) high and across.

Most widely grown are aptly named mophead and lacecap varieties of *Hydrangea macrophylla*. Yielding pink, mauve or red blooms on alkaline soils and blue heads in acid conditions, they thrive in fertile ground. Characteristically, lacecaps have an outer ring of large, sterile flowers enclosing tiny, pink or blue, fertile ones.

Other choice kinds are white, football-headed *H. arborescens* 'Annabelle' and light pink, cone-flowered *H. paniculata* 'Pink Diamond'. *H. quercifolia* has oak-leaved foliage which complement trusses of rich creamy flowers and *H. villosa* is a gem with porcelain-blue mushrooms poised above stems clad with huge, velvety leaves.

A self-clinging climber, white, disc-flowered *H. petiolaris* beautifully transforms a cold, north-facing wall.

CONDITIONS

Aspect Dappled sunlight or morning sun and afternoon shade suit hydrangeas. Make sure they are sheltered from frosty winds, which will damage embryo blossoms. *H. macrophylla* varieties are reliable seaside plants for relatively frost-free areas.

Site These shrubs need damp soil high in organic matter, so improve poor areas by digging in plenty of well-decayed manure or compost a few months ahead of planting. Also mulch plants with well-rotted organic matter.

GROWING METHOD

Feeding Apply acidifying fertiliser like sulphate of ammonia in spring and midsummer to ensure a steady release of plant foods and encourage blue flowers.

Propagation Multiply favoured varieties by layering flexible shoots from mid-spring to late summer. Take soft-tip cuttings from late spring to early summer and semi-ripe cuttings from mid- to late summer.

Problems Excessive lime prevents chlorophyll from forming and causes leaves to yellow and die. Overcome it by applying iron chelates.

PRUNING

H. macrophylla: Cut off spent flowers in spring and remove crowding shoots.

H. paniculata: Prune stems to within two buds of the base in late March.

H. petiolaris: Cut out unwanted shoots when flowers fade.

H. villosa: Remove a third of older stems in spring.

HYDRANGEA AT A GLANCE

Deciduous shrubs bearing large heads of white, pink, red or blue flowers from mid- to late summer. Hardy to -15°C (4°F).

		RECOMMENDED VARIETIES
JAN	/	
FEB	/	Mopheads
MAR	plant, prune	'Hamburgh'
APR	plant, prune	'Madame E. Moullière'
MAY	plant	Lacecaps
JUNE	plant	'Blue Wave'
JULY	flower, plant	'White Wave'
AUG	flower, plant	*H. arborescens* 'Annabelle'
SEPT	flower, plant	*H. paniculata* 'Kyushu'
OCT	plant	*H. quercifolia*
NOV	plant	*H. villosa*
DEC	/	

HYDRANGEA VARIETIES

RIGHT: 'Kyushu', a dashing paniculata variety, highlights late summer and autumn with a shuttlecock of shoots topped with pyramidal sprays of starry blossom.

ABOVE: 'Masja' luxuriates in damp soil and treats us to a memorable display of deep red to purplish-red 'mopheads'. Group it with white-flowering Anemone *'Honorine Jobert'.*

LEFT: Unlike other hydrangeas, dramatically white-flowered Hydrangea quercifolia *has large, oak-like leaves, which develop striking orange tints in October.*

ABOVE: Impressive 'Générale Vicomtesse de Vibraye' is an easy variety to 'blue' in neutral to acid soils. Apart from using proprietary chemicals, you can transform blooms from pink to blue by working rusty metal into the root area.

BELOW: Exquisite lacecap varieties have a central dome of small fertile flowers embraced by a ring of large, handsome, sterile florets.

RIGHT: Seeking a deep red and free-flowering mophead? Opt for 'Gerda Steiniger', whose clustered heads make August and Sepember special.

JASMINE
Jasminum

Illuminating a north or east-facing wall from November to March, Jasminum nudiflorum *flowers very freely on cascading shoots.*

Ideal for clothing a pergola or trellis work, twining Jasminum officinale affine *is swathed with scented flowers in summer.*

FEATURES

There are two forms of jasmine – climbing and bushy – both of which flower generously. Choice and reliable twining climbers – ideal for screening – are *Jasminum affine*, to 7.5m (25ft), whose pink buds open to sweetly scented, white flowers from July to September; and *J.* × *stephanense*, to 4.5m (15ft), which from early to midsummer pleases with a profusion of perfumed, pale pink blooms amid colourful, cream-flushed, green leaves.

Among bushy kinds, the popular, yellow-flowered winter jasmine (*J. nudiflorum*) is usually trained to transform a wall or fence from November to late February. After establishing a main framework, leave it to flower freely on cascading shoots. Aspiring to half that height, semi-evergreen *J. humile* 'Revolutum' is dashingly clad with larger, fragrant, yellow blossoms from late spring to autumn. Even smaller is yellow-flowered,

mound forming *J. parkeri*, which when planted on a rock garden brightens it in early summer.

CONDITIONS

Aspect
While climbing kinds need a sheltered spot and full sunshine for most of the day, the most popular bushy member – *G. nudiflorum* – thrives on a shaded, north wall lashed by frosty winds.

Site
Undemanding, all flourish on most well-drained soils. Enrich and improve the water retention of thin, sandy areas by digging in bulky organics several months before planting. Help clay drain better by forking in gravel.

GROWING METHOD

Feeding
Give young plants a good start by consigning them to generous planting holes fortified with bone meal or Growmore fertiliser. Soak the soil after planting to settle it around roots and remove air pockets. Encourage robust growth by working bone meal into the root area in spring and autumn.

Propagation
Layer whippy shoots from spring to late summer or take semi-ripe cuttings from mid- to late summer.

Problems
Grey mould, a fungus covering leaves with a greyish, furry patina, may occur if shoots are crowded. Control it by removing affected parts and spraying with carbendazim.

PRUNING

Climbing kinds are not normally cut back. If they outgrow their situation, shorten shoots after flowering. Keep *J. nudiflorum* youthful and massed with bloom by removing a third of the older flowered stems when flowers fade in early spring.

JASMINE AT A GLANCE

Semi-evergreen or deciduous, twining or bush forms colour walls and fences in winter and summer. Hardy to -15°C (4°F).

JAN	flower	
FEB	flower	
MAR	prune	**RECOMMENDED VARIETIES**
APR	plant	
MAY	flower, plant	*J. affine*
JUN	flower, plant	*J. humile* 'Revolutum'
JULY	flower, plant	*J. nudiflorum*
AUG	flower, prune	*J. parkeri*
SEPT	flower, plant	*J.* × *stephanense*
OCT	plant	
NOV	plant	
DEC	/	

KERRIA
Kerria japonica

A charmingly tangled mass of bright yellow flowers in spring makes kerria an attractive screening plant, even at dusk.

Kerria has single or double flowers and leaves that develop radiant yellow tints in autumn. This is the double 'Pleniflora' version.

FEATURES

Graceful and arching, deciduous *Kerria japonica* makes a fascinating focus to about 1.8m (6ft) high. From April to May, its radiant orange-yellow blooms clothe a profusion of suckering, cane-like, green stems. Coveted forms are 'Pleniflora', magnificent with its double, golden pompons; 'Golden Guinea', with beautiful, single, buttercup-yellow flowers; and smaller 'Picta' – just 90cm (3ft) high – whose single, yellow blossoms complement cream-edged, green leaves. Very hardy and happy almost anywhere, taller kinds making dense and colourful hedges.

CONDITIONS

Aspect   This shrub flowers best in full sun and performs passably well in shade.
Site   Kerria will thrive almost anywhere.

GROWING METHOD

Feeding   Keep growth vigorous and packed with blossom in spring by applying bone meal in March and October. Water new plants frequently to help them establish quickly.
Propagation   Probably the easiest shrub to multiply, it can be increased from semi-ripe cuttings in midsummer; layered shoots from mid-spring to late summer; hardwood cuttings in late autumn; and suckers in early spring.
Problems   No particular pests or diseases.

PRUNING

Cut out from the base a third of older shoots when blooms fade in early summer. Remove green-leaved stems on variegated bushes.

KERRIA AT A GLANCE

Deciduous shrub with green stems dotted with single or double, yellow blooms in spring. Hardy to -25°C (-13°F).

		RECOMMENDED VARIETIES
JAN	/	
FEB	/	'Albescens'
MAR	plant	'Golden Guinea'
APR	flower, plant	'Picta'
MAY	flower, plant	'Pleniflora'
JUNE	plant, prune	'Simplex'
JULY	plant	
AUG	plant	
SEPT	plant	
OCT	plant	
NOV	plant	
DEC	/	

LAVENDER
Lavandula

Blooming from July to September, evergreen lavender excels in free-draining 'hot spots'. Make sure you get the plant you want by buying it in flower.

Aromatic French lavender is a delightful cottage-garden plant. Brush against it and citrus scent fills the air.

FEATURES

Never out of fashion, hardy, evergreen lavender forms a rounded shrub 30–75cm (12–30in) high. From July to September, its aromatic, grey-green foliage complements spikes of tightly clustered, pale blue, purple, pink or white flowers. Interplant it with other shrubs or border perennials or set it to form a fetching divide between open-plan gardens. Choice varieties are: dwarf, compact and rich purple-blue 'Hidcote'; equally neat, lavender-blue 'Munstead'; and taller French lavender (*Lavandula stoechas* 'Papillon'), the dark purple flowers of which are borne in dense, lozenge-shaped heads. Flowers are used fresh in posies and dried for pot-pourri or cosmetics. Lavender is an archetypal cottage-garden plant. Its common names of French, English or Italian lavender apply to different species, but even experts find it hard to agree upon which is which.

LAVENDER AT A GLANCE

Aromatic, greyish-leaved evergreen with scented, lavender, purple, pink or white flowers in summer. Hardy to -10°C (14°F).

		RECOMMENDED VARIETIES
JAN	/	
FEB	/	'Hidcote'
MAR	/	'Loddon Pink'
APR	plant, prune	'Munstead'
MAY	plant	'Nana Alba'
JUNE	plant	'Twickel Purple'
JULY	flower, plant	*L. vera*
AUG	flower, plant	*L. stoechas* 'Papillon'
SEPT	flower, plant	
OCT	/	
NOV	/	
DEC	/	

CONDITIONS

Aspect Lavender needs an open situation in full sun with good air circulation. Do not crowd it with other plantings.

Site Thriving on most well-drained soils, it prefers coarse, sandy or gravelly loam. Lime acid soils before planting.

GROWING METHOD

Feeding Boost growth of young plants by topdressing the root area with fish, blood and bone meal in spring and midsummer. When established, after two years, no regular fertilising is necessary.
Water new plantings copiously to help them recover quickly. When well established, lavender is seldom stressed by droughty spells.

Propagation Take semi-ripe cuttings from early to mid-autumn. Alternatively, work sharp sand into the crown in spring, watering it well, so lower branches are buried. Detach rooted layers in autumn and move them to their new positions.

Problems Lavender is seldom troubled by pests or diseases but may succumb to root rot in heavy or overwet soils. If crowded, in sheltered gardens, the foliage may die back. Remove dead growth and thin out stems to improve air circulation.

PRUNING

Use shears to trim dead blooms from bushes and hedges after flowering.
Rejuvenate older, 'tired' plants and help them bloom freely by shortening the previous year's flowered stems to new shoots within 5–10cm (2–4in) of the base. Do this from early to mid-spring. Never cut back into older wood, for it seldom regenerates and plants may die.

LAVENDER VARIETIES

RIGHT: Create a feature by interplanting 'Sawyers', a robust and deep purple-flowered variety, with Perovskia *'Blue Spire', a Russian sage with greyish-white-stemmed spikes of rich blue flowers.*

ABOVE: Thriving in a warm, sunny border, French lavender (Lavandula stoechas) forms an appealing globe to 60cm (2ft) high and across. A wealth of lozenge-shaped flower heads in summer, and leaves, emit a strong citrus scent.

LEFT: Seeking a small, white variety for a patio pot? Opt for 'Nana Alba'. Just 20cm (8in) high, it associates stunningly with a fringe of trailing, purple Surfinia petunias.

BELOW: An archetypal cottage-garden plant, old English lavender (Lavandula angustifolia) makes a handsome fountain of blossom to 90cm (3ft) high.

BELOW: Keen to plant a low lavender hedge to flank a path or driveway? Plump for 'Munstead', whose thickly clustered shoots are topped with dark lavender-blue flowers.

NEW ZEALAND TEA TREE

Leptospermum scoparium

Smothered with tiny, disc-like blooms from May to June, Leptospermum *'Red Damask' is best fan-trained against a warm, sunny wall in all but very mild areas.*

Keep tea tree youthful and glowing with blossom by removing a third of the older shoots when flowers fade.

FEATURES

Bejewelled from May to June with stalkless, disc-like blooms amid small, narrow leaves, twiggy and slender, purplish-stemmed *Leptospermum scoparium* is an evergreen worth caring for. Forming a rounded bush, 1.8–2.4m (6–8ft) high, it is usually grown against a sheltered wall. Alternatively, set it among other shrubs that shield it from biting winds. Trained as a mini-standard, it makes a fetching feature for a sun-soaked patio. Favoured varieties are double 'Red Damask', single, clear pink 'Huia' and double, white 'Snow Flurry'. Be warned: tea trees may be short-lived unless conditions are ideal.

TEA TREE AT A GLANCE

A slightly frost-tender evergreen, it is studded with tiny, red, pink or white blooms from May to June. Hardy to -5°C (23°F).

		RECOMMENDED VARIETIES
JAN	/	
FEB	/	'Huia'
MAR	/	'Kiwi'
APR	plant	'Red Damask'
MAY	flower, plant	'Snow Flurry'
JUNE	flower, plant	
JULY	plant, prune	
AUG	plant	
SEPT	plant	
OCT	/	
NOV	/	
DEC	/	

CONDITIONS

Aspect
Leptospermum needs full sun and protection from chilly, north or east winds. Ideally fan-train it against a south- or west-facing wall. Make sure air freely circulates to reduce risk of mildew felting and crippling leaves.

Site
The planting area must be well drained. Improve light, sandy soils by digging in old manure or well-rotted garden compost.

GROWING METHOD

Feeding
Encourage robust flowering growth by applying an acidifying fertiliser in spring and midsummer. Water young plants regularly in their first year after planting. Thereafter, soak the root area periodically in dry periods and mulch with shredded bark.

Propagation
Multiply plants from soft-tip cuttings in June or semi-ripe cuttings in late summer.

Problems
Plants are susceptible to root rot in clay soils. Avoid it by forking in grit or gravel before planting. Webbing caterpillars, such as lackey moth, can cause leaves to drop. Cut off and destroy egg bands or webbed shoots and spray with permethrin, bifenthrin or fenitrothion.

PRUNING

If leptospermum outgrows its allotted space, remove one shoot in three from the base, when flowers fade in midsummer. Do not cut back into older wood as it seldom re-grows. Remove straggly shoots in spring.

HONEYSUCKLE

Lonicera

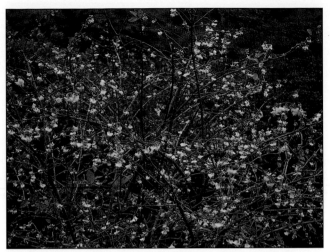

Small and bushy Lonicera fragrantissima *treats us to a massed display of vanilla-perfumed, creamy flowers from mid- to late winter.*

Clothed with sweetly scented blooms from June to October, Lonicera japonica *'Halliana' makes a fetching screen for a sunny patio.*

FEATURES

A trio of sweetly scented, bushy honeysuckles worth cultivating are: *Lonicera fragrantissima*, with its vanilla-perfumed, creamy-white, bell-shaped blooms, which are freely borne on twiggy shoots to 1.8m (6ft) from January to March; slightly smaller *L. x purpusii*, which treats us to a similar display from November to March; and *L. syringantha*, with its profusion of clustered, lilac flowers on 90cm (3ft) stems from late spring to early summer. Twining varieties, trained to frame a door or clothe a wall, fence, arbour, pergola or arch or to scramble through a tree, enhance a garden. Colour spring by planting yellow and red *L. periclymenum* 'Belgica' and continue the show – from June to October – with white and red *L.p.* 'Serotina'.

CONDITIONS

Aspect   Plant lonicera in full or lightly dappled shade to grow strongly and flower freely.

Site   These shrubs and climbers prefer well-drained and humus-rich, sandy loam or clay loam but also tolerate chalky soil. Improve light soils, which dry out quickly, by working in bulky organic materials well before planting.

GROWING METHOD

Feeding   Speed robust growth and a panoply of blossom by enriching the root area with bone meal in spring and autumn.
Water liberally to encourage young plants to establish quickly. Once growing strongly, all varieties are unstressed by droughty periods. In spring, mulch thickly with humus-forming organics to keep roots cool and questing and encourage a fine display of blossom.

Propagation   Take hardwood cuttings in late autumn or
Shrubs: early winter, or layer whippy stems from mid-spring to late summer.
Climbers: Take semi-ripe cuttings from early to midsummer.
Problems   Blackfly are attracted to new shoots, which they quickly smother. Control them with pirimicarb, natural pyrethrins, bifenthrin or horticultural soap.

PRUNING

Keep winter-flowering *L. fragrantissima* and *L. x purpusii* shapely and full of young shoots, which flower freely, by removing one stem in three in mid-spring. Help spring- and early summer-blooming *L. syringantha* prosper by cutting back flowered shoots to new growth when blooms fade.
Prune *L. periclymenum* varieties and *L. japonica* 'Halliana' by shortening flowered stems to new shoots when blooms fade.

HONEYSUCKLE AT A GLANCE

Semi-evergreen bushes and deciduous and evergreen climbers light up spring, summer and winter. Hardy to -25°C (-13°F).

		RECOMMENDED VARIETIES
JAN	flower	
FEB	flower	Bushes
MAR	plant	*L. fragrantissima*
APR	flower, prune	*L. x purpusii*
MAY	flower, prune	*L. syringantha*
JUNE	flower, prune	*L. tartarica*
JULY	flower, plant	Climbers
AUG	flower, prune	'Belgica'
SEPT	flower, prune	*L. heckrottii* 'Goldflame'
OCT	plant	'Serotina'
NOV	plant	*L. japonica* 'Halliana'
DEC	/	*L. tragophylla*

MAGNOLIA
Magnolia

Unfolding in March and April, before leaves appear, starry-flowered Magnolia stellata *lights up dappled shade.*

Planted to contrast with a dark green-leaved shrub, the star magnolia makes a statement. Underplant it with blue-flowered grape hyacinths.

FEATURES

Heralding spring, *Magnolia stellata*, a deciduous, bushy shrub to around 2.1m (7ft), illuminates borders with a multitude of fragrant, strap-petalled, starry, white flowers from March to April. Also called star magnolia, it is ideal for small gardens. Fetching varieties are pink-budded, white-flowered 'Royal Star', white-flowered 'Centennial', whose blooms are 14cm (5.5in) across, and Waterlily', another handsome, white variety with flared, double chalices that command close attention.

Most other magnolias, such as evergreen *M. grandiflora*, which flowers best if fan-trained on a sunny, sheltered wall, and varieties of *M. soulangeana*, soar to around 4.5m (15ft).

MAGNOLIA AT A GLANCE

White or pink flowers are thickly borne on leafless branches in early spring. *M. stellata* is hardy to -25°C (-13°F).

JAN	/	
FEB	/	
MAR	flower, plant	
APR	flower, plant	
MAY	flower, prune	
JUN	plant, prune	
JULY	plant, flower*	
AUG	plant, flower*	
SEPT	plant, flower*	
OCT	/	
NOV	/	
DEC	/	

RECOMMENDED VARIETIES

*M. grandiflora**
M. grandiflora 'Heaven Scent'*
M. grandiflora 'Little Gem'*
M. soulangeana 'Lennei'
M. soulangeana 'Picture'
M. stellata
M. stellata 'Centennial'
M. stellata 'Royal Star'

* summer flowering

CONDITIONS

Aspect No matter how large or small the variety, magnolias should be sheltered from strong winds. To flower well, they must receive at least half a day's sunshine.

Site *M. stellata* and *M. grandiflora* prosper in well-drained, acid, neutral or alkaline soil. *M. soulangeana* abhors chalk. Dig in plenty of organic matter well ahead of planting.

GROWING METHOD

Feeding Encourage bountiful blooms by applying an acidifying fertiliser – brands for azaleas and camellias are ideal – in April and July.

Propagation Take soft-tip cuttings from late spring to early summer. Increase *M. grandiflora* from semi-ripe cuttings in midsummer.
Layering is more reliable but takes longer. Peg down shoots from spring to late summer and detach rooted stems a year later in autumn.

Problems Soft, unfolding leaves can be scorched by hot, dry or salty winds, so position plants carefully.

PRUNING

Seldom necessary. If a shrub requires shaping or crowded branches need removing, tackle it when flowers fade in mid-spring. Never prune in winter, as corky tissues are liable to rot.

MAGNOLIA VARIETIES

RIGHT: A glorious sight in May, a mature bush of Magnolia soulangeana *'Alba Superba' is massed with upright, tulip-like, snow-white blossoms, purple at the base. Site it carefully – in a sheltered, sunny spot free from frost, which reduces blooms to soggy mops.*

ABOVE: Showered in spring with goblet-shaped blooms, rosy purple outside, suffused cream and purple within, Magnolia soulangeana *'Lennei' treats us to a further, smaller display in autumn.*

LEFT: A Japanese gem, Magnolia liliiflora *'Nigra' rewards us with a multitude of long, slender, candle-like buds that open to deep purple blooms stained creamy white and purple within. When mature, petals reflex and become starry. As well as planting it in the garden, set it in a large, well-drained patio tub in which it will grow slowly and flower bounteously.*

BELOW: A good choice for a small garden, Magnolia stellata *makes a neat globe to around 1.5m (5ft) high after ten years or so. It is very accommodating, does not need pruning and is seldom attacked by pests or diseases.*

RIGHT: A hybrid raised at the US National Arboretum, Washington, Magnolia liliiflora × stellata *'Judy' is one of several hybrids superior to their parents in flower size, profusion of blossom, colour and scent.*

MAHONIA
Mahonia

Tall, bushy mahonias display shuttlecocks of citrus-scented, pale lemon to golden flowers from early winter to early spring. Decorative, blue berries follow in autumn.

Mahonia x media 'Charity' illuminates a dry, shady spot from mid- to late winter.

FEATURES

Ground-hugging, weed-suppressing and good for stabilising steep banks, tall and sculptural, evergreen mahonias have shiny, spiky, holly-like leaves that develop burnished coppery or reddish tints in winter. Flamboyant, citrus-scented heads of yellow or golden-clustered, slender, cone-like flowers appear from November to May. Blooms are followed by decorative, bluish-black berries. From 60cm (2ft) to 2.4m (8ft) high, depending on the species, taller kinds make fetching focal points, dense screens or dashing background plants. Varieties of suckering, ground-covering *Mahonia aquifolium*, which thrives in light shade, effectively carpet rooty areas around trees and shrubs. Position orb-shaped and free-flowering *M. x media* 'Charity' and more upright 'Lionel Fortescue' to light up winter.

CONDITIONS

Aspect	Thriving in sun or dappled shade, mahonias resist cold winds.
Site	These shrubs flourish in all but very chalky conditions. Improve poor soils by adding bulky organic matter several weeks before planting.

GROWING METHOD

Feeding	Boost growth by working fish, blood and bone meal or Growmore into the root area in mid-spring and midsummer. If they are growing where there is root competition, mulch thickly to help conserve moisture.
Propagation	Raise species from seeds in early to mid-spring, in a garden frame. Take leaf-bud cuttings in mid-autumn or mid-spring and root in a heated propagator. Divide *M. aquifolium* into well-rooted portions in mid-spring.
Problems	Control mahonia rust by spraying with penconazole, mancozeb, or bupirimate with triforine. *M. aquifolium* and *M. bealei* have some resistance to this disease.

PRUNING

M. aquifolium:	Prevent plants from becoming leggy by removing one stem in three after flowering.
Tall, bushy hybrids:	Remove flower heads when blooms fade; rejuvenate old, gaunt plants by shortening stems by half their height in May.

MAHONIA AT A GLANCE

Carpeting or upright evergreens, with holly-like leaves, colour borders from November to March. Hardy to -25°C (-13°F).

JAN	flower	RECOMMENDED VARIETIES	
FEB	flower		
MAR	flower	*M. aquifolium* 'Apollo'	
APR	flower, plant	*M. aquifolium* 'Atropurpurea'	
MAY	prune, flower	*M. aquifolium* 'Smaragd'	
JUNE	plant	*M. japonica*	
JULY	feed	*M. lomariifolia*	
AUG	plant	*M. x media* 'Charity'	
SEPT	plant	'Lionel Fortescue'	
OCT	plant	'Winter Sun'	
NOV	flower		
DEC	flower		

SACRED BAMBOO
Nandina domestica

Nandina's autumn bounty of bright red berries follows a summer display of white flowers. Leaves are greenish but tinted cream, pink, orange and red.

Unlike true bamboo, the sacred version is light, airy and not invasive and is ideal for colonising a restricted space.

FEATURES

Reminiscent of bamboo, nandina is a slender-stemmed evergreen that slowly spreads by suckers to make a fascinating focal point. Grown for its brightly hued, cream, orange, pink and red leaves, its 'airy' shoots create an impression of 'lightness'. Nandina, much prized for Japanese-style gardens, may also be sited elsewhere to contrast effectively with darker-toned and heavier-textured plants. Small, white flowers from June to July are followed by attractive, red berries, which linger into autumn. Makes a handsome bush to 1.2m (4ft) high by 90cm (3ft) across.

SACRED BAMBOO AT A GLANCE

Bamboo-like evergreen whose cream-, orange- and pink-tinted leaves complement white flowers. Hardy to -10ºC (14ºF).

		RECOMMENDED VARIETIES
JAN	/	
FEB	/	'Firepower'
MAR		'Nana Purpurea'
APR	plant	'Richmond'
MAY	prune	
JUNE	plant, flower	
JULY	plant, flower	
AUG	plant, flower	
SEPT	plant	
OCT	/	
NOV	/	
DEC	/	

CONDITIONS

Aspect   Thriving in full sun or semi-shade, it needs shielding from chilly winds, which can blacken leaves. Ideally, plant it at the foot of a south- or west-facing wall.

Soil   Nandina prefers well-drained and humus rich, sandy loam. Augment chalk or heavy clay soils with bulky organic materials a month or two before planting.

GROWING METHOD

Feeding   Encourage luxuriant foliage and large clusters of fruit by working bone meal into the root area in spring and autumn.
Once established, nandina is fairly drought resistant. Mulch with well-rotted garden compost, manure, shredded bark or cocoa shell in spring to insulate roots from moisture-extracting sunshine.

Propagation   In autumn, extract seeds from ripe berries, sow in pots and raise in a garden frame. Take semi-ripe cuttings from mid- to late summer. Use a spade to split up large clumps in mid-spring.

Problems   Severe winter weather may kill shoots to ground level and new growth from roots may be slow in appearing.

PRUNING

No regular cutting back is necessary. Rejuvenate old clumps in May by removing a third of the older stems at ground level.

OLEANDER
Nerium oleander

Delighting us with white, yellow, apricot, pink or crimson blooms from spring to autumn, evergreen but poisonous oleander is easy to grow.

Create a Mediterranean tapestry by grouping a pot-grown oleander next to a spiky-leaved yucca and scarlet pelargonium.

FEATURES

Frost-tender and principally a conservatory plant, evergreen oleander enjoys a summer airing on a sunny, sheltered patio or terrace. Depending on variety, it makes a handsome shrub, 1.2–1.8m (4–6ft) high. Sumptuous heads of white, yellow, pink, apricot, cerise or scarlet, single or double blooms appear from June to November. Thrusting, upright stems are clad with slender, leathery leaves. Oleanders are long-lived and flower early in life. Choice varieties include: semi-double, light pink 'Clare'; single, apricot 'Madame Leon Blum'; double, white 'Soeur Agnes'; and single, deep red 'Hardy's Red'. Double, pink-flowered 'Variegatum', with cream or yellow-rimmed leaves, is very popular with flower arrangers. The plant is poisonous if eaten.

OLEANDER AT A GLANCE

Studded with showy blooms in many glowing hues, frost-tender oleander is usually grown in a conservatory. Hardy to 7°C (45°F).

		RECOMMENDED VARIETIES
JAN	/	
FEB	/	'Clare'
MAR	plant	'Emile'
APR	plant, prune	'Géant des Batailles'
MAY	flower, plant	'Luteum Plenum'
JUNE	flower, plant	'Professor Granel'
JULY	flower, plant	'Soeur Agnes'
AUG	flower, plant	'Soleil Levant'
SEPT	flower, plant	'Variegatum'
OCT	flower	
NOV	flower	
DEC	/	

CONDITIONS

Aspect
Oleander needs full sun and shelter from cold winds to prosper and flower freely. Only in frost-free gardens can it be grown outdoors all year round. Elsewhere, grow it in a pot indoors – in a lounge or conservatory – and move it outside when frosts finish in late May.

Site
This shrub thrives in most free-draining soil types but abhors heavy, waterlogged clay. If growing it in a large pot or tub, set it in proprietary tub or hanging basket compost.

GROWING METHOD

Feeding
Border plants: Encourage large clusters of blossom by sprinkling bone meal over the root area in spring and autumn and hoeing it in. Tub grown (indoors in winter): Insert slow-release fertiliser granules into the compost in spring. Repot root-bound plants in spring. Though oleander tolerates long, dry periods, soak roots occasionally in hot, dry weather.

Propagation
Raise plants from seeds sown in a heated propagator in spring or take semi-ripe cuttings in midsummer.

Problems
If plants are attacked by limpet-like scale insects, control them by spraying two or three times, fortnightly, with malathion or horticultural soap.

PRUNING

Keep oleander youthful and blooming freely by shortening flowered shoots by half their length when blossoms fade. Ensure plants stay neat and bushy by shortening side shoots to 10cm (4in) in spring.

OSMANTHUS
Osmanthus

Forming an umbrella of small, evergreen shoots, Osmanthus delavayi's *thickly clustered, tubular flowers sleeve shoots in spring.*

A beacon of bright, cream-rimmed, evergreen leaves from Osmanthus heterophyllus 'Variegatus' *illuminates dull, winter days.*

FEATURES

An easy, enchanting and small, glossy, leathery-leaved evergreen from western China and Japan, osmanthus forms an orb of shoots and colours spring and autumn.

Light up April and May with *Osmanthus x burkwoodii*. Growing to around 1.8m (6ft) high by 1.2m (4ft) across, its toothed, pointed leaves foil slender stems massed with clusters of small, white, vanilla-fragrant, tubular blooms. Create a riveting feature by grouping it with orange or yellow deciduous azaleas. It also makes a dense, wind-proof hedge.

Closely related *O. delavayi* is another spring-flowering treasure. Arching to 1.5m (5ft) high, it too is smothered with bunches of small, white blooms that spill jasmine perfume on to the air. Small, black fruits follow them.

Later, from September to October, comes taller *O. heterophyllus*, to 3m (10ft) high and across, the soft leaves of which deceive you into thinking it is a form of holly. It does a sterling job in colouring the closing year with a profusion of tiny, white blossoms. Its coloured-leaved varieties – purple 'Purpureus' and creamy 'Aureomarginatus' – are stunning throughout the year.

CONDITIONS

Aspect All, apart from *O. delavayi* which is best grown again against a sheltering, warm wall in chilly districts, thrive in the open.

Site If possible, set plants in free-draining, humus-rich soil that does not dry out or become waterlogged. Fortify sandy or chalky soils with bulky organic manure.

GROWING METHOD

Feeding Boost growth by sprinkling Growmore or some other balanced fertiliser over the root area in spring, repeating in midsummer. Water it in if the soil is dry. Foliar feed in droughty spells, when roots have difficulty absorbing plant foods, to speed uptake of nutrients. Water new plants copiously and follow with a mulch of bark, cocoa shell or well-rotted garden compost.

Propagation Increase varieties by layering flexible shoots from late spring to late summer or take semi-ripe cuttings from mid- to late summer.

Problems Seldom attacked by pests or diseases.

PRUNING

No regular cutting back is necessary. If awkward shoots need removing, do it in spring when flowers have finished. Shorten stems to just above a joint or to new shoots. Trim a hedge of *O. x burkwoodii* when flowers fade in May.

OSMANTHUS AT A GLANCE

Spring- or autumn-flowering evergreens for sun or light shade, *O. x burkwoodii* makes a stocky hedge. Hardy to -5°C (23°F).

		RECOMMENDED VARIETIES
JAN	/	
FEB	/	*O. x burkwoodii*
MAR	/	*O. delavayi*
APR	flower, plant	*O. heterophyllus*
MAY	flower, plant	*O. heterophyllus* 'Aureomarginatus'
JUNE	prune	
JULY	/	*O. heterophyllus* 'Purpureus'
AUG	/	*O. heterophyllus* 'Variegatus'
SEPT	flower, plant	
OCT	flower	
NOV	/	
DEC	/	

MOCK ORANGE
Philadelphus

Semi-arching 'Belle Etoile' is thickly clothed with richly vanilla-scented, single, large, white and flushed-yellow blooms from June to July.

Plant soaring Philadelphus lemoinei *'Erectus' to brighten a sunny spot with a myriad perfumed blooms sleeving upright shoots.*

FEATURES

Often but erroneously called syringa – the correct name for lilac – its sumptuous, creamy white, single or double and richly citrus-vanilla-scented blooms fill and brighten the high-summer gap, when the spring display of shrubs is fading and autumn contenders have yet to form flower buds. Ranging in height from 60cm (2ft) to over 3m (10ft), there are candidates for most situations.

Coveted tall varieties, 1.8–3m (6–10ft), are: large, single and pink-centred 'Beauclerk'; semi-double and yellowish-white *Philadelphus coronarius*; and double or semi-double, pure white 'Virginal'. Couple flowers with striking foliage by planting semi-double, creamy white *P. coronarius* 'Aureus', the leaves of which open lemon-yellow and mature to greenish yellow. This plant is perfect for lighting up a sunny or dappled shady border.

Set the smallest member, 'Manteau

d'Hermine', just 60–90cm (2–3ft) high, on a rock garden and enjoy its massed, double, creamy white blossoms. Taller kinds are good for hedging.

CONDITIONS

Aspect
Ideal for windswept, hillside gardens and for tolerating salty breezes, mock orange thrives almost anywhere. All flower best in full sun and lemon-leaved *P. coronarius* 'Aureus' keeps its radiant leaf colour in light shade.

Site
Thriving in most soils – acid sand, chalk or heavy clay – it is best to enrich poor patches with bulky organic matter dug in several months before planting.

GROWING METHOD

Feeding
Encourage bounteous blossom on sandy soil by applying annually sulphate of potash in late winter and late summer. Regardless of soil, topdress the root area with a balanced fertiliser in April and July.
In a dry spring, water regularly to encourage strong, new shoots, which will flower the following year.

Propagation
Strike cuttings of semi-ripe shoots from mid- to late summer. Root them in a cold frame or on a sunny windowsill.

Problems
Blackfly can colonise and cripple soft shoot tips. Control them by spraying with pirimicarb, which does not harm beneficial insects.

PRUNING

When blooms fade, cut back flowered shoots to current-year stems, which will perform the following year.

MOCK ORANGE AT A GLANCE

A deciduous shrub whose single or fully double, creamy white flowers appear from June to July. Hardy to -25°C (-13°F).

		RECOMMENDED VARIETIES
JAN	/	
FEB	/	Under 1.8m (6ft)
MAR	plant	'Belle Etoile'
APR	plant	*Coronarius* 'Aureus'
MAY	plant	'Manteau d'Hermine'
JUNE	flower	'Sybille'
JULY	flower	Over 1.8m (6ft)
AUG	prune	'Beauclerk'
SEPT	/	*Coronarius*
OCT	plant	'Virginal'
NOV	plant	
DEC	/	

PHOTINIA
Photinia

The awakening year sees Photinia fraseri *draped with clusters of tiny, white flowers, occasionally followed by red berries.*

In spring and early summer, Photinia 'Red Robin' *is a beacon of shining maroon-scarlet leaves. Here it is contrasting with an apple-green hebe.*

FEATURES

A valued New Zealand evergreen to around 1.8m (6ft) high by 1.5m (5ft) across, *Photinia* x *fraseri* 'Red Robin' is a visual delight. From mid- to late spring, a foam of fluffy, white flowers, sometimes followed by scarlet berries, complements brilliant red, shiny leaves that mature to green. Riveting in a winter-colour border, it is also appealing when fan-trained against a sunny, sheltered wall or fence. Alternatively, plant it in a large pot or tub and train it as a globe, pyramid or drumstick. Clip trained forms in spring and summer. Photinia also makes a dense, low hedge.

PHOTINIA AT A GLANCE

The most popular kind, *P.* x *fraseri* 'Red Robin', enchants us with a wealth of scarlet, new leaves. Hardy to -15ºC (4ºF).

		RECOMMENDED VARIETIES
JAN	/	
FEB	/	'Birmingham'
MAR	/	'Red Robin'
APR	flower, plant	'Robusta'
MAY	flower, prune	'Rubens'
JUNE	flower, plant	
JULY	plant	
AUG	plant	
SEPT	plant	
OCT	/	
NOV	/	
DEC	/	

CONDITIONS

Aspect Not the hardiest of shrubs, photinia prefers a sheltered, sunny situation in which its foliage colours magnificently. It tolerates light shade.

Site This shrub thrives on most well-drained soils but hates heavy clay and chalk. Improve sandy patches by incorporating bulky organic manures several weeks before planting.

GROWING METHOD

Feeding Encourage stocky shoots and lustrous leaves by topdressing the root area with fish, blood and bone meal, or some other balanced fertiliser, in spring and midsummer.
Water young plants copiously in dry spells in their first year to initiate strong, new shoots.

Propagation Layer young stems from spring to late summer; take semi-ripe cuttings in late summer.

Problems Photinia is susceptible to apple scab, a fungus that causes leaves to develop greyish-green spots and fall early. Control it by raking up diseased leaves, pruning out and burning scabby shoots and spraying with carbendazim, mancozeb or bupirimate with triforine.

PRUNING

Rejuvenate old, leggy bushes by shortening stems by a third of their length in mid-spring. Remove shoot tips periodically throughout spring and summer, to encourage flushes of new, red leaves.

PIERIS
Pieris

Young pieris leaves open a vivid shade of pink or scarlet before turning yellow and ultimately green.

Some varieties, such as 'Wakehurst', not only produce scarlet, flower-bright leaves but also combine them with an unstinting display of lily-of-the-valley-like blossom.

FEATURES

A captivating, evergreen shrub, 40cm–2.7m (16in–9ft) high and across, its bell-shaped, white, pink or red flowers glorify spring. Its other, equally prized asset is its glowing pink or reddish shuttlecocks of new leaves. There are many varieties. Aptly named 'Flaming Silver' – 60cm (2ft) high, ideal for a narrow border – has fiery, new leaves which when mature are suffused with silver.

PIERIS AT A GLANCE

New, red, evergreen leaves complement sprays of white, pink or red, bell-shaped flowers in spring. Hardy to -10°C (14°F).

JAN	/	
FEB	/	
MAR	flower	RECOMMENDED VARIETIES
APR	flower, plant	'Debutante'
MAY	flower, prune	'Firecrest'
JUNE	plant, prune	'Flaming Silver'
JULY	plant	'Forest Flame'
AUG	plant	'Mountain Fire'
SEPT	plant	'Pink Delight'
OCT	/	'Valley Valentine'
NOV	/	
DEC	/	

CONDITIONS

Aspect Not a candidate for exposed gardens, pieris needs shielding from strong, chilly winds and hot, leaf-scorching sunshine.

Site Abhorring any degree of lime, this shrub needs deep, rich, well-drained soil. Create a good home for it by digging in generous amounts of organic material well ahead of planting time.

GROWING METHOD

Feeding Boost robust growth by applying an acidifying fertiliser in spring and midsummer. Help young plants recover quickly from transplanting by watering regularly in droughty spells and mulching with moisture-conserving organics.

Propagation Multiply plants by pegging down low shoots from mid-spring to late summer or take semi-ripe cuttings from mid- to late summer.

Problems New leaves may be damaged by wind frost.

PRUNING

Cut off faded blooms and dead or damaged shoots in early summer. Rejuvenate old bushes by shortening gaunt shoots to half their height in mid-spring. Keep cuts moist in dry spells to encourage rapid regrowth.

SHRUBBY CINQUEFOIL
Potentilla fruticosa

Forming a spreading clump, 'Red Ace' – riveting when interplanted with Artemisia *'Powis Castle' – fires a border from May to October.*

Prized for its display of butter-yellow flowers, 'Dart's Golddigger' contrasts stunningly with rosy-pink bedding geraniums.

FEATURES

Potentilla fruticosa flowers continuously from late May to September, its small, saucer-shaped blossoms clustering on dense, wiry stems.

Carpeting or bushy, to 1.5m (5ft) – taller kinds making colourful hedges – it is hardy and a good choice for cold gardens.

Easy, eye-catching varieties are: greyish-green-leaved and white-flowered 'Abbotswood'; creamy-yellow 'Tilford Cream'; ground-covering 'Dart's Golddigger'; chrome-yellow 'Goldstar'; salmon-pink 'Pretty Polly'; vermilion-flame 'Red Ace'; and deep orange to brick-red 'Sunset'.

All are good contenders for patio and terrace tubs and pots or deep, generous windowboxes. Arrange a potted group in several harmonising colours to flank a doorway or form a focal point at the end of a path. Shrubby cinquefoil can also be grown to embrace pergola posts.

SHRUBBY CINQUEFOIL AT A GLANCE

Deciduous, bushy plants, which also make good hedges, they flower from May to September. Hardy to -25°C (-13°F).

		RECOMMENDED VARIETIES
JAN	/	
FEB	/	Carpeting
MAR	plant	'Dart's Golddigger'
APR	plant, prune	'Pretty Polly'
MAY	plant, flower	'Red Ace'
JUNE	plant, flower	'Sunset'
JULY	plant, flower	Bushy
AUG	plant, flower	'Goldfinger'
SEPT	plant, flower	'Goldstar'
OCT	plant, flower	'Red Robin'
NOV	plant	'Tilford Cream'
DEC	/	

CONDITIONS

Aspect A good choice for borders exposed to chilly winds, shrubby cinquefoil flowers profusely in an open, sunny position or very light shade. If possible, plant it facing south or west where trees will not overshadow it.

Site A very adaptable plant, it thrives in most soils, from heavy, often waterlogged clay to light, sandy areas that become parched in summer. It does not mind a little lime but on very chalky soils it is liable to become stressed and suffer from chlorosis, when leaves turn creamy or yellowish and die.

GROWING METHOD

Feeding Encourage robust flowering shoots by working fish, blood and bone meal or some other balanced fertiliser into the root area in spring and midsummer. Apply bone meal in autumn to release plant foods in spring. If, in sandy soil, leaf margins turn brown, indicating potash deficiency, rectify by applying sulphate of potash in February and watering it in. Once the plant is established, watering is seldom needed, but soak newly planted shrubs to settle the soil around the roots.

Propagation Increase plants from cuttings of semi-ripe shoots in midsummer. Root them in a garden frame or on a sunny windowsill.

Problems Shoots produce their leaves very late in spring, deceiving us into thinking them dead.

PRUNING

Keep bushes youthful and flowering freely year after year by removing a third of the older shoots in spring. Rejuvenate very old, woody plants at the same time by cutting them back to within 10cm (4in) of the base. Trim hedges in spring.

CAPE LEADWORT
Plumbago

Commonly called Cape leadwort, plumbago rewards us with a succession of silvery-blue flowers from mid- to late summer.

Encourage plumbago to flower bounteously every year by shortening the previous year's flowered stems in February.

FEATURES

Usually grown to colour a conservatory, greenhouse or windowsill with a mist of starry, sky-blue flowers from midsummer to autumn, *Plumbago auriculata* is a rambling, evergreen climber. Ideally, grow it in a large pot or tub to allow you to move it on to a patio when frosts finish in late May or early June. Growing to 4.5m (15ft) or so, in cultivation it is best pruned regularly to keep it neat, compact and floriferous. In very sheltered, frost-free gardens, create a sensation in summer by training it over an arch, arbour, obelisk or trellis.

CAPE LEADWORT AT A GLANCE

Scrambling, frost-tender climber studded with pale blue flowers from midsummer to early autumn. Hardy to 8°C (46°F).

		RECOMMENDED VARIETIES
JAN	/	
FEB	prune	*P. auriculata*
MAR	/	*P. auriculata alba*
APR	plant	'Royal Cape'
MAY	plant	
JUNE	plant	
JULY	flower	
AUG	flower	
SEPT	flower	
OCT	flower	
NOV	/	
DEC	/	

CONDITIONS

Aspect Though plumbago flowers best in full sun, it tolerates very light shade.

Site Set this shrub in a large, well-drained pot or small tub of multi-purpose compost.

GROWING METHOD

Feeding Insert clusters of slow-release fertiliser granules into the compost in spring. From late spring to summer, apply a high-potash tomato feed.
When potting plants, add moisture-storage granules to help keep the compost damp during long, dry spells.
In late summer, when nights turn chilly, return plumbago to a frost-free spot in good light. Keep the compost dryish from autumn to spring.

Propagation Take semi-ripe cuttings from early to midsummer.

Problems Under glass, fluffy, waxy, white mealy bugs may colonise leaf joints and cripple growth. Control them biologically with *Aphidius colemani*, a parasitic wasp, or spray with horticultural soap.

PRUNING

Shorten the previous year's flowering shoots to within 5cm (2in) of the older wood in February.

ORNAMENTAL CHERRY
Prunus

From early to mid-spring, a wealth of disc-shaped, double pink blooms transform Prunus x blireana*'s bare, twiggy branches.*

Heralding spring and suitable for all sizes of garden, white-, pink- or red-flowering cherries associate beautifully with magnolias.

FEATURES

Deciduous or evergreen shrubs or trees 1.2–4.2m (4–14ft) tall, the prunus family embraces a wide range of forms. Flowers are single or double, in white, pink and red shades. Neat dwarf Russian almond (*Prunus tenella* 'Firehill') has semi-double, rosy-crimson flowers, which sleeve 1.2m (4ft) stems in April. Also useful for small gardens is *P.* x *cistena* 'Crimson Dwarf', whose white flowers appear just before coppery-red leaves. White-flowering and low-growing evergreen kinds – *P.* 'Otto Luyken' among them – are excellent for carpeting shady spots. Taller laurel (*P. laurocerasus* 'Rotundifolia') makes a dense evergreen hedge to 1.8m (6ft).

ORNAMENTAL CHERRY AT A GLANCE

A huge family of deciduous, spring-flowering cherries and carpeting or hedging evergreens. Hardiness rating, according to species.

JAN	/	
FEB	/	RECOMMENDED VARIETIES
MAR	plant, flower	Evergreen
APR	prune, flower	'Otto Luyken'
MAY	flower, plant	*P. laurocerasus*
JUNE	plant, flower	'Rotundifolia'
JULY	plant, prune	'Zabeliana'
AUG	plant, prune	Deciduous
SEPT	plant	'Amanogawa'
OCT	plant	*P.* x *blireana*
NOV	plant	'Cheal's Weeping'
DEC	/	*P. mume*
		P. tenella 'Firehill'

CONDITIONS

Aspect   Deciduous flowering cherries, needing full sun to perform well, should be sheltered from strong winds. Evergreens thrive in light shade.

Site   All prunus prosper on any well-drained soil enriched with organic matter. Evergreen varieties also thrive on thin, sandy soils.

GROWING METHOD

Feeding   Work bone meal into the root area in spring and autumn. Water freely in dry spells, especially when flower buds are forming.

Propagation   Increase evergreen, carpeting and hedging varieties from semi-ripe cuttings from mid- to late summer. Flowering cherry trees, however, are normally grafted on to *P. avium* rootstock.

Problems   Control silver leaf disease by cutting back and burning affected shoots to 15cm (6in) beyond infected, purple-stained tissue, in midsummer.

PRUNING

Evergreens: Shear laurel hedges in spring and late summer.

Deciduous varieties: No regular pruning is necessary. Cut out crowding shoots from mid- to late summer.

CHERRY VARIETIES

ABOVE: Pale pink blooms that open white and contrast with dark reddish-purple leaves make Pissard's purple plum (Prunus cerasifera 'Pissardii') a desirable garden tree. Red fruits follow in summer.

ABOVE: Prunus and malus flowers are very similar. This Malus 'John Downie' could be mistaken for a flowering cherry.

LEFT: Enchanting in a small border, Prunus triloba treats us to massed rosettes of pale pink blooms that cluster on year-old shoots in April. Keep it youthful and blooming freely by pruning out one stem in three in early summer.

BELOW: A snowfall of single, white blooms smothers Prunus 'Taihaku' in May. Position it in full sun, in a large lawn, where it can develop fully without having to be cut back. Alternatively, set it near a contrasting, deep green hedge to accentuate the whiteness of its flowers.

ABOVE: Famed for its profusion of white, candle-like blooms in spring and again in autumn, Prunus 'Otto Luyken' is also prized for its ground-hugging, evergreen and weed-suppressing leaves. It flourishes in sun or shade.

POMEGRANATE
Punica

Showy, bell-shaped, orange-scarlet flowers are your reward for growing a pomegranate in a warm garden or conservatory.

Delicious fruits appear on outdoor or patio pot plants after a long, warm summer. Under glass, in a higher temperature, fruits swell to a greater size.

FEATURES

Deciduous and bearing carnation-like, single or double, brilliant orange-red flowers for most of the summer, *Punica granatum* makes a bushy shrub to 2.1m (7ft) high and across. Only single-flowered varieties bear fruits. Grow them as specimen plants in very sheltered borders in frost-free gardens. Elsewhere, treat this shrub as a pot plant and confine it to a conservatory from autumn to late spring. Move it on to a sunny patio or terrace when frosts finish in late May or early June.

POMEGRANATE AT A GLANCE

Deciduous and bearing orange flowers in summer, it can be grown outside only in very sheltered areas. Hardy to 4°C (39°F).

JAN	/	
FEB	/	RECOMMENDED VARIETIES
MAR	/	'Flore Pleno Luteo'
APR	plant, prune	'Flore Pleno Rubro'
MAY	plant, prune	*P. granatum nana*
JUNE	flower, plant	'Striata'
JULY	flower, plant	
AUG	flower, plant	
SEPT	plant	
OCT	/	
NOV	/	
DEC	/	

CONDITIONS

Aspect   If you are growing pomegranate outdoors, it must be in full sunshine and protected from cold winds.

Site   To excel, this shrub needs well-drained loam or clay-loam soil enriched with humus-forming organics.

GROWING METHOD

Feeding   Boost growth and stimulate plenty of blossom-bearing shoots by applying bone meal in spring and autumn.
Encourage young plants to establish quickly by watering liberally in the first spring and summer after planting.
In September, return potted plants that have decorated a patio for summer to a frost-free conservatory or greenhouse.

Propagation   Increase this plant from semi-ripe cuttings taken from mid- to late summer.

Problems   New shoots on outdoor plants can be damaged by late spring frosts, so site the shrubs carefully.

PRUNING

Remove badly placed shoots from late spring to early summer. Keep wall-trained specimens shapely by shortening flowered shoots to within four leaves of the main framework when blooms fade.

FIRETHORN
Pyracantha

A spectacular autumn display of orange, red or yellow berries, following a foam of creamy blossom, makes firethorn popular for transforming cold walls.

Planted to screen out ugly objects, firethorn's late-season bonanza of berries is a welcome winter feast for garden birds

FEATURES

Planted mainly for screening, hedging and training as an espalier, evergreen and hardy firethorn's spiky stems are clad with small, glossy green leaves. In early summer, showy clusters of white flowers, appearing early in the plant's life, are followed by a dramatic cloak of bright orange, yellow or red berries from autumn to winter. Garden birds feast on them. There are many long-lived varieties. Choice kinds include a trio of recently bred fireblight-resistant forms: orange-berried 'Saphyr Orange'; red-berried 'Saphyr Red'; and yellow-berried 'Saphyr Yellow'. These shrubs grow 1.8–3m (6–10ft) high, which they reach after 5–10 years.

FIRETHORN AT A GLANCE

An evergreen shrub coveted for its white flowers and display of red, orange or yellow berries. Hardy to -25°C (-13°F).

		RECOMMENDED VARIETIES
JAN	/	
FEB	/	'Alexander Pendula'
MAR	/	'Dart's Red'
APR	plant, prune	'Golden Charmer'
MAY	plant	*P. rogersiana*
JUNE	flower, plant	'Saphyr Orange'
JULY	plant	'Saphyr Red'
AUG	plant	'Saphyr Yellow'
SEPT	plant	
OCT	/	
NOV	/	
DEC	/	

CONDITIONS

Aspect Needing full sun for healthy, compact growth, firethorn flowers less and is more loosely branched in light shade. It tolerates strong gusts and is often grown as a windbreak.

Site Tolerating a wide range of soil types including chalk, it prefers well-drained loam or clay-loam enriched with organic matter. It also prospers on humus-rich, gravelly patches.

GROWING METHOD

Feeding Keep firethorn lustrous and flowering and berrying freely by working bone meal into the root area in spring and autumn.
Help newly planted shrubs establish quickly by watering copiously in dry spells during their first spring and summer. Mulch thickly.

Propagation Take semi-ripe cuttings from mid- to late summer.

Problems Disfiguring leaves and berries with patches, pyracantha scab is a debilitating disease.
Control it by pruning out and burning infected shoots and spraying fortnightly with carbendazim from March to July. Grow orange-red berried 'Mohave', which is resistant to it.

PRUNING

Free-standing shrubs: Cut back overgrown plants in April to keep them flowering and berrying profusely.

Wall-trained espaliers: In spring, shorten non-blossoming side shoots to 10cm (4in) from the base. In midsummer, reduce current-year shoots to three leaves.

RHODODENDRON
Rhododendron

Few shrubs can equal rhododendrons for a spectacular display of blossom from late winter to summer. This skillfully planned garden features a bold planting of white and rosy-red hardy hybrids framed by dark foliage that enhances rather than competes with the flowers.

FEATURES

Enriching gardens with spectacular trusses of vibrant or delicate pastel-hued blooms from December to August, there is an enormous range of evergreen and deciduous varieties. Without doubt, they are the key to creating fetching features on acid soil.

Yielding thickly or sparsely clustered, bell- or trumpet-shaped blooms, rhododendrons are long-lived and mature within 5–10 years. Plant them to enhance woodland glades, borders, rock gardens, patio pots and conservatories. Associate them with other lime-hating plants, such as azaleas, Japanese maples, lilies, camellias, conifers, eucryphia, pieris and embothrium.

TYPES

Hardy hybrids: Valued for their resistance to severe weather and ability to prosper in windy gardens, hardy hybrids flower from April to June. Most grow 1.5–2.4m (5–8ft) high and across.
They are easy to manage and the blooms, in white and shades of red, pink, lavender, purple and yellow, are borne in large, showy trusses amid broad, pointed leaves.

Red hues: Outstanding are: ruby red 'Bagshot Ruby'; bright brick-red 'Vulcan'; bright red, black-speckled 'Windlesham Scarlet'; dark red 'Doncaster', black-veined within; and medium-red 'Cynthia'.

Pink hues: A trio no garden should be without is: dark green-leaved and rose-pink 'Alice'; 'Pink Pearl', whose rosy buds open to flesh-pink blooms; and 'Furnivall's Daughter', a gem with rose-pink and dark-spotted flowers.

Purple, blue and mauve hues: Stunning among these are: violet-blue 'Blue Boy'; semi-double and bluish-mauve 'Fastuosum Flore Pleno'; and rosy-purple 'Variegatum', whose white-rimmed leaves illuminate shady places.

White hues: White and pale yellow-eyed 'Cunningham's White' and lavender-budded and white-flowered 'Loder's White' light up mid-spring.

RHODODENDRON AT A GLANCE

Evergreen shrubs mantled with blooms from late winter to midsummer. All need acid soil. Hardiness ratings vary.

		RECOMMENDED VARIETIES
JAN	/	
FEB	flower	Hardy hybrids
MAR	flower	'Doncaster'
APR	flower, plant	'Furnivall's Daughter'
MAY	flower, prune	'Pink Pearl'
JUN	flower, prune	'Fastuosum Flore-Pleno'
JULY	plant	'Cunningham's White'
AUG	plant	'Praecox'
SEPT	/	Yakushimanum hybrids
OCT	/	'Astrid'
NOV	/	'Chelsea Seventy'
DEC	/	'Grumpy'

TOP: *Sun-loving, hardy hybrid 'Blue Peter'.*
ABOVE: *An exquisite-flowered Vireya rhododendron.*

A 19th-century Malaysian variety used for breeding, 'Pink Delight' is spectacular for a shaded conservatory or very mild, frost-free garden, but it needs cosseting.

Low-growing varieties: Equally hardy, low-growing varieties make dense bushes 45–120cm (18–48in) high. Heralding spring, 'Praecox' opens its rosy-lilac-to-mauve blooms in February and March; 'Snow Lady' bears lovely, white flowers from March to April; and 'Princess Anne' is smothered with clear yellow blooms from April to May.

Stunning, too, are drought-resisting hybrids of *Rhododendron yakushimanum*. Making dense bushes to 90cm (3ft), alluring varieties are: cerise-pink 'Astrid'; salmon and carmine-rose 'Chelsea Seventy'; and yellowish-white and shell-pink 'Grumpy'.

The sumptuous and very colourful Malaysian (Vireya) rhododendrons make exciting focal points for a frost-free greenhouse or lightly shaded and very sheltered patio or terrace in summer.

CONDITIONS

Aspect Hardy hybrids and species grow and flower best in a dappled, shady spot shielded from strong wind.

Site Soil must be acid and well-drained, cool and moist throughout the year and fortified with moisture-conserving organic matter. Dig in plenty of well-rotted manure, garden compost or leaf mould before planting. Set greenhouse varieties in large pots of orchid-bark, mixed with ericaceous compost.

GROWING METHOD

Feeding Nourish plants with an acidifying fertiliser in spring and midsummer and mulch thickly with bulky organic materials to keep roots active and leaves lustrous in long, dry spells.

Use lime-free rain water to moisten dry soil or compost.

Propagation Take softwood cuttings from mid-spring to early summer and semi-ripe cuttings in early autumn; layer stems from mid-spring to late summer.

Problems *Bud blast: This fungus turns flower buds brown and is characterised by bristly black outgrowths, is spread by rhododendron leaf hopper. This is also a pest, which lays its eggs in the bud scales. Control bud blast by picking off and burning affected buds and spraying with pirimiphos-methyl to eradicate hoppers.
*Leaf spot disease: Speckling leaves with brownish-purple spots containing raised, black, fungal fruiting bodies, it is best eradicated by spraying with mancozeb when symptoms appear.
If aphids colonise soft shoot tips, control them with pirimicarb, which is selective to this pest and does not harm beneficial insects.
*Lime-induced chlorosis: Caused by a deficiency of iron and manganese in alkaline soils, which inhibits chlorophyll production, leaves develop brown rims and yellow patches between bright green veins. Rectify it by applying a chelated compound based on iron, manganese and other trace elements.

PRUNING

Snap off spent blooms when petals fall, to channel energy away from seed production and into strong new growth. Take care not to damage new leaves.

Keep mature bushes youthful and packed with blossom in spring by removing one in three of older, black-barked stems when flowers fade. Dwarf and low-growing varieties and species are best left unpruned.

AZALEA
Rhododendron

Planted to light up a woodland glade, evergreen Kurume azalea 'Kirin' treats us to a massed display of small blooms in May.

Leaf-shedding Mollis azaleas yield an unforgettable display of large clusters of vibrantly hued, trumpet blooms before leaves fully unfold.

FEATURES

Enchanting us from April to June, deciduous and evergreen azaleas come in a kaleidoscope of colours and range in height, 60cm–2.4m (2–8ft). They are derived from various species of rhododendron and are among the world's most widely hybridised plants. Long-lived, azaleas mature within 3–5 years and flower from the first year of planting. Grouped in mixed shrub borders, taller varieties make a stunning backcloth for annuals or small perennials. It is best to buy plants in flower so that you can be sure of getting exactly what you want. Azaleas are often planted with acid-soil-loving camellias and purple- and green-leaved Japanese maples, where the foliage tempers the more vibrant-hued varieties.

Deciduous groups: Cherished for their May to June performance of clustered, trumpet blooms in glowing pastel and strident hues and vivid autumn leaf tints, there are four deciduous types:

Mollis hybrids: Making stocky bushes to about 1.8m (6ft) high, their large heads of scentless, bright yellow, orange, red, cream and salmon blooms open before leaves appear. Choice among them are orange-scarlet 'Spek's Brilliant' and 'Koster's Brilliant Red'.

Knaphill and Exbury hybrids: Also unperfumed, their May blooms can be as large as a hardy hybrid rhododendron's. Dramatic varieties are: light yellow 'April Showers'; salmon-pink 'Coronation Lady'; and deep carmine 'Homebush'.

Ghent hybrids: Making neat, twiggy bushes clothed in long-tubed, sweet-smelling, honeysuckle-like flowers with showy stamens, blossoms peak in late May and June. Fine forms are soft yellow 'Narcissiflorum' and rose-pink 'Norma'.

Occidentalis hybrids: Flowering from mid- to late May, they reward us with trusses of sumptuous, fragrant, pastel-hued blooms. Pure white and yellow-eyed 'Bridesmaid' is a good example.

Evergreen and semi-evergreen groups: There are four widely grown divisions. Largest flowering are the prolific Vuyk and Glendale hybrids, whose blooms can be 7.5cm (3in) in diameter. The Kaempferi hybrids, such as violet 'Blue Danube', have slightly smaller flowers.
Smallest of all are the very popular and bounteous-performing Kurume hybrids. These have slightly greater tolerance to low temperatures than other evergreen varieties and blooms are single or hose-in-hose – when one flower appears inside another.

AZALEA AT A GLANCE

A form of deciduous or evergreen rhododendron bearing trumpet blooms, it colours lightly shaded spots. Hardy to -15°C (4°F).

		RECOMMENDED VARIETIES
JAN	/	
FEB	/	Deciduous
MAR	plant, prune	'Bridesmaid'
APR	flower, prune	'Coronation Lady'
MAY	flower, prune	'Firefly'
JUN	flower, prune	'Gibraltar'
JULY	plant	'Koster's Brilliant Red'
AUG	plant	Evergreen
SEPT	plant	'Addy Wery'
OCT	plant	'Blue Danube'
NOV	plant	'Driven Snow'
DEC	/	'Hinode-giri'

CONDITIONS

Aspect Most azaleas prefer semi-shade and shelter from strong winds and hot afternoon sunshine. A new race of 'sun-loving' varieties is being

RIGHT: Too tender for planting in the garden, though they benefit from spending June to September in a cool, shaded spot outdoors, Indica azaleas are massed with blossom from December to February.

BELOW: Complementing the hardy varieties' spring display, this glowing, half-hardy Indica azalea is unusual in that it has a clearly defined, white centre.

RIGHT: Deciduous Mollis azaleas come in vivid shades of orange yellow. This beautiful variety, flowering from early to mid-May, associates dramatically with pieris while it is displaying its scarlet, new leaves.

VARIETIES

LEFT: Few azaleas can surpass the brilliance of 'Happy Days', a prized but rare Nuccio hybrid, the double flowers of which illuminate spring. Shield young plants from frost.

BELOW: Lighting up May and June, deciduous azaleas – this is a Mollis variety – reward us with clusters of flared-petal blooms and elegant thrusting stamens.

LEFT: This free-flowering Glenn Dale hybrid is one of many varieties bred to improve the frost-hardiness and colour range of evergreen azaleas.

A riot of spring blossom in yellow, orange and other sunny shades makes it worthwhile finding a choice site for a Mollis azalea.

bred for more open situations, but it could be some years before they are listed by British specialists.

Site
The soil should be acid, well-drained and humus-rich and fortified with plenty of well-decayed organic matter several weeks before planting. In even slightly alkaline conditions, when the pH hovers just above 7.0, azaleas will suffer from iron deficiency and creamy-green, chlorophyll-deficient leaves will die. Keep plants perky in hot spells by mulching with a thick layer of organic material, such as well-rotted manure, leaf mould, compost or decayed grass clippings.

GROWING METHOD

Feeding
Nourish plants by applying an acidifying fertiliser in spring and summer and watering it in if the soil is dry.
Water new plants regularly in droughty periods to help them establish quickly. In prolonged dry weather, gently dig a moat around a bush and fill it with water. Refill it several times when the water has soaked away. Finish by replacing the soil.

Propagation
Azaleas are easily increased from soft-tip cuttings taken from mid-spring to early summer; semi-ripe cuttings from mid- to late summer; and layers pegged down from mid-spring to late summer.

Problems
Unfortunately azaleas suffer from a number of pests and diseases.
*Powdery mildew: Causing yellow patches to blemish upper leaf surfaces it can, occasionally, trouble heavily shaded plants in areas of high rainfall. It can also be aggravated by sluggish air flow, so remove crowded plants and set them elsewhere. Pick off and burn badly affected leaves and avoid wetting the foliage. Do not grow *Rhododendron cinnabarinum* or its

hybrids, which are prone to this fungus. Control the disease chemically by spraying with bupirimate with triforine or mancozeb the moment symptoms appear.
*Azalea gall: Blame the fungus *Exobasidium vaccinii*, which causes leaves to become swollen, fleshy and pinkish red. Later, ripe, white spores powder the surface. In autumn, galls wither and turn brown. Fortunately, the plant does not appear to suffer from its presence. Some varieties are more susceptible than others to azalea gall. Remove and destroy affected leaves. There are no chemical controls.
*Rhododendron lace bug damages azalea and rhododendron leaves in spring, summer and into autumn in mild seasons. Affected foliage is heavily mottled greyish white. Black or brown, shiny spots, the insect's excreta, are seen on the underside of leaves. When damage first appears, it may be possible to reduce the outbreak by hosing up under the foliage; otherwise, spray with horticultural soap, pyrethrins, pirimiphos-methyl or permethrin as soon as the symptoms are seen.
*Thrips – brownish black and 2mm (⅛in) long – suck sap from the leaves. The damage is similar to that of lace bug but the leaves may have a more silvery appearance. Control these pests by spraying with pirimiphos-methyl, malathion or dimethoate. If the infestation is severe, in dry, warm weather when thrips multiply rapidly, you may need to repeat the dosage every three weeks.
*Two-spotted mite, commonly known as red spider mite, also sucks sap from the underside of leaves. Using a magnifying glass, it is possible to see the mites. Almost colourless, with two black spots on their backs, they are usually carrying clear, round eggs.
An attack is first noticed when leaves turn bronzy, tiny webs can be seen and minute creatures, with the aid of a hand lens, can be seen on the backs of leaves. Mites are more prevalent in hot, dry weather and more inclined to infest plants in sheltered spots, such as under eaves, than in open, airy situations. If the plants are not in flower when red spider mite invades, direct a hose up into the bush every couple of days to help reduce their numbers. Alternatively, spray with bifenthrin or horticultural soap.

PRUNING

Cutting flowers for a vase is usually all the pruning these plants need. But deadhead, too, to channel energy into new growth, by nipping out faded blooms when petals fall. Rejuvenate overgrown deciduous varieties by cutting back branches to within 60cm (2ft) of the ground in March, before buds burst. Try and keep cuts moist to keep alive invisible buds around the stump edge. An easy way to achieve this, apart from splashing them with water, is to coat them with Christmas tree needle spray, which covers them with a plastic film that seals in moisture. If the bush is very old, prune back half the branches in the first year and the remainder the following year. Wayward stems may be cut back at any time.

FLOWERING CURRANT
Ribes

Blooming generously from April to May, sun-loving Ribes 'Pulborough Scarlet', a flowering currant, also performs in light shade.

Trained against a warm wall and almost evergreen, the fuchsia-flowered currant (Ribes speciosum) *makes a fascinating feature.*

FEATURES

A deciduous family that heralds spring, the most popular kind – *Ribes sanguineum* 'Pulborough Scarlet' – is very hardy. Growing to around 2.4m (8ft) high and 1.8m (6ft) across, its upright shoots are thickly sleeved with pendent clusters of deep red, tubular flowers. 'White Icicle', another choice form of *R. sanguineum*, has drooping, creamy-white candelabra blooms, dramatic when embraced with purple-red *Bergenia* 'Evening Glow'. *Ribes sanguineum* 'Brocklebankii', to 1.2m (4ft), is illuminatingly different, rewarding us with a heartening display of golden leaves and pink flowers. All varieties of *R. sanguineum* can be planted to form a stocky, flowering boundary hedge.
Starry, yellow-flowered *R. odoratum*, to 1.8m (6ft), has leaves that assume purple tints in autumn, and less hardy *R. speciosum*, prized for its scarlet, fuchsia-like flowers on upright spiny shoots and best grown against a warm wall, are also generous performers.

CONDITIONS

Aspect Ribes is ideal for brightening a lightly shaded spot, but *R.* 'Brocklebankii' must be shielded from hot sunlight otherwise its leaves will scorch. All, apart from slightly tender *R. speciosum*, prosper in exposed gardens. Make a statement by espalier training *R. speciosum* against a warm, sunny wall or set it to cascade from a pedestal pot.

Site Undemanding ribes thrives almost anywhere. Fortify sandy spots, which parch in summer, with bulky, moisture-conserving organics. If you plant this shrub on heavy clay, add gravel to improve drainage. Chalky soils can cause leaves to become chlorotic (yellowish green). Avoid this by adding acidifying fertiliser to lower the pH level.

GROWING METHOD

Feeding Provided the soil is reasonably fertile, a single application of bone meal in autumn is all that is necessary. After planting, no matter how damp the ground, water well to settle soil around the roots.

Propagation Take hardwood cuttings in late autumn.
Problems This genus is prone to coral spot fungus. Causing a rash of coral-pink or orange pustules that kills shoots, it should be controlled by cutting out and burning infected plant tissue. Remove crowded shoots to improve air flow.

PRUNING

Keep ribes youthful, shapely and flowering freely by shortening a third of older shoots to new growth or near ground level when blooms fade. Remove crowding branches and cut back diseased stems to healthy wood in spring.

FLOWERING CURRANT AT A GLANCE

Deciduous bush festooned with clusters of flowers from late March to mid-May. Hardiness rating according to species.

		RECOMMENDED VARIETIES
JAN	/	
FEB	/	*R. odoratum*
MAR	flower, plant	*R. sanguineum* 'Brocklebankii'
APR	flower, plant	
MAY	flower, plant	*R. sanguineum* 'Icicle'
JUN	plant, prune	*R. sanguineum* 'Porky Pink'
JULY	plant	
AUG	plant	*R. sanguineum* 'Pulborough Scarlet'
SEPT	plant	*R. speciosum*
OCT	/	
NOV	/	
DEC	/	

ROSE
Rosa

A sport of the famous 'Peace' rose, 'Chicago Peace' is a vibrant Large Flowered variety that forms a stocky bush to 1.2m (4ft) high.

For sheltered, frost-free gardens, there are few more wonderful sights than the Cherokee rose (Rosa laevigata) draping a sunny wall.

FEATURES

For over two millennia, roses have played an important role in garden design. However, it was not until the 19th century, from an amalgam of new developments – Hybrid Musk, Hybrid Perpetual and Large Flowered (Hybrid Tea) roses – that modern varieties evolved. Since the late 1960s, there has been great interest in what are known as 'English' roses. Bred by David Austin, they are varieties that combine the many-petalled form, lovely fragrance and full vigour of an old-fashioned rose with the wide colour range and repeat-flowering qualities of a modern rose.

Roses are cherished for their form and colourful blooms, and many are very fragrant. They can be evergreen or deciduous, and most varieties have prickles.

The Old Roses – varieties of *Rosa gallica*, beloved by the Greeks and Romans; Damasks, alleged to have been introduced from the Middle East by the Crusaders; Albas, grown by gardeners in the Middle Ages; and Centifolias, first seen in Britain around 1550, which flower just once, in early summer.

Modern roses – Cluster Flowered (Floribunda), Large Flowered (Hybrid Tea) produce successive flushes of bloom. Flowers may be single, semi-double or fully double, in a wide range of colours: white, cream, yellow, apricot, orange, every shade of pink and red. There are bicolours, too, but a true blue rose has yet to be borne. Weed-suppressing and ideal for covering banks too steep to mow, the County Series of ground-hugging roses, such as blush-pink 'Avon', gold, cerise, pink and scarlet 'Cambridgeshire' and pure white 'Kent', colour summer with repeat pulses of bloom. Ramblers, including coppery pink and richly scented 'Albertine' flower only in midsummer. Climbers particularly modern varieties, such as 'Golden Showers', salmon-pink 'Compassion'

and honey-champagne 'Penny Lane', have Hybrid Tea-like flowers and bloom repeatedly from June to October.

Some species, such as *R. moyesii*, produce brilliant red hips in autumn and are planted specially for these, although the flowers are good too!

Uses Roses may be mass-planted in beds and borders or planted singly as sentinels. Large Flowered, Cluster Flowered and some other bush varieties are also grown as round-headed or weeping standards to flank a path or add height to a bed of roses. Thrusting through an obelisk strategically positioned in a shrub border, 'Handel', a short, creamy-white and rose-pink climber, makes a riveting focal point.

Climbers and ramblers also associate strikingly with pink, red, blue and white varieties of *Clematis viticella*, which are pruned to within 30cm (12in) of the base in spring. Create a sensation by planting violet-blue C. 'Etoile Violette' to entwine the climbing rose 'Compassion', whose fragrant, double, light salmon-shaded, orange blooms stud strong, healthy shoots all summer.

Miniature and patio roses are ideal for planting in pots or tubs to decorate a patio or terrace. Very hardy varieties of *Rosa rugosa* are often used as hedges. Set a Large Flowered or Cluster Flowered variety *en masse* to illuminate a bed or border, or embrace a single bush with annuals, perennials or bulbs.

CONDITIONS

Aspect The hardiness of roses is variable. Many tolerate extreme cold while others can be singed by frost.

To form stocky shoots and flower bounteously, roses need full sun all day. Good air circulation is important, too, but some shelter from strong wind is desirable to avoid flower damage.

Site These shrubs prefer heavy but well-drained,

Flowering profusely in early summer and sporadically thereafter, leggy 'Felicia', a Hybrid Musk, is ideal for screening eyesores.

humus-rich loam. Improve light, sandy, gravelly or chalky soils by adding large amounts of well-rotted manure or decomposed garden compost several few weeks before planting. Add garden lime to very acid soil.

GROWING METHOD

Feeding Encourage lustrous leaves and fine, large blooms by feeding with a proprietary rose fertiliser, containing magnesium, in mid-April and early July.

Propagation Vigorous Cluster Flowered varieties, most shrub roses and ramblers and climbers are easily increased from hardwood cuttings in September. The only way to multiply Large Flowered varieties is to implant a bud of the variety, in July, on to a rootstock.

Problems *Aphids, which are sap suckers, may cover new growth quite thickly. Spray with pirimicarb, horticultural soap, permethrin, pirimiphos-methyl or derris.
*Leaf-rolling sawfly damages roses from late spring to early summer. When females lay eggs on leaves, they inject a chemical into the leaf, which causes it to roll up and protect the eggs. Affected leaflets hang down. When caterpillars emerge, they feed on the leaves. Control with heptenophos, permethrin or pirimiphos-methyl.
*Black spot causes large black blotches to disfigure leaves. Collect and burn fallen leaves and avoid overhead watering. Some roses are less prone to this disease than others. Resistant Large Flowered varieties: 'Alec's Red', 'Alexander', 'Blessings', 'Champs Elysees', 'Chicago Peace', 'Honey Favourite'. Resistant Cluster Flowered varieties: 'Allgold', 'Arthur Bell', 'City of Belfast', 'City of Leeds', 'Manx Queen', 'The Queen Elizabeth', 'Tip Top'.
*Powdery mildew, worse in dry spots and where air circulates sluggishly, distorts leaves,

stems and flower buds and felts them with greyish-white patches.
Control it by opening up crowded areas, watering and liquid feeding every ten days, from spring to late summer, with a high-potash fertiliser to encourage robust growth. Also guard against infection by spraying fortnightly from spring to late summer, with triforine with bupirimate, penconazole, mancozeb or copper with ammonium hydroxide.
*Rust is another fungus that is worse in areas of high rainfall. In early summer, bright orange spots appear on the upper leaf surface and corresponding, orange spore clusters disfigure the lower surface. In late summer, dark brown winter spore masses replace summer pustules. Badly infected leaves are shed prematurely. Control rust by pruning out and burning affected stems and spraying regularly with myclobutanil, penconazole, bupirimate with triforine or mancozeb.

PRUNING

Tackle pruning in early spring before buds burst. In autumn, shorten extra long stems on bush roses to avoid them catching the wind and loosening the stem. Always cut to just above a bud.

After planting: Large Flowered and Cluster Flowered bush varieties: Shorten stems to within 15cm (6in) of the base.
Shrub roses: No pruning necessary.
Ramblers: Cut back shoots to 30cm (12in) from the ground.
Climbers: Shorten withered tips to healthy buds.

When established: Large Flowered and Cluster Flowered: Shorten main stems by half their length; side shoots to two buds.
Shrub roses: Cut back dead and dying shoots to healthy buds.
Ramblers: Most varieties are pruned in autumn; cut out flowered stems and replace with current-year shoots.
Climbers: Shorten flowered side shoots to two or three buds.
Deadhead all roses weekly to channel energy into new shoots and more flowers.

ROSE AT A GLANCE

Bushes, standards, weepers, carpeters and climbers flower from spring to autumn. Most roses are hardy to -16°C (3°F).

		RECOMMENDED VARIETIES
JAN	/	
FEB	/	Large Flowered
MAR	plant, prune	'Alec's Red'
APR	plant, prune	'Elizabeth Harkness'
MAY	flower, plant	English roses
JUN	flower, plant	'Graham Thomas'
JULY	flower, plant	Cluster Flowered
AUG	flower, plant	'English Miss'
SEPT	flower, plant	Patio roses
OCT	flower, plant	'Sweet Dream'
NOV	plant	Climbers
DEC	/	'Breath of life'

ROSE

LEFT: A Large Flowered and upright grower to 1.2m (4ft), richly scented 'Double Delight' was introduced from America around 20 years ago. Its popularity has never waned.

RIGHT: Associating roses with other plants is an exciting challenge. Here this sumptuous Cluster Flowered variety is harmonising with Crambe cordifolia blossom.

BELOW: Because they absorb light, it is vital to plant scarlet and other deeply hued roses in a bright, sunny spot. In even light shade, blooms tend to disappear on dull days.

RIGHT: A vigorous and healthy bush to 90cm (3ft), 'Sunblest' is a profuse Large Flowered variety. Strong stems are topped with tightly formed buds that open to reveal unfading bright yellow blooms.

VARIETIES

LEFT: Though lacking the impact of semi- and fully double Large Flowered roses, single-flowered Polyantha varieties have innate charm and flower for months.

ABOVE: 'Bernina', a Cluster Flowered rose yet to come to Britain, was developed for and named after the Swiss sewing machine company. It bears a multitude of scented and perfectly formed flowers.

LEFT: Appealing to flower arrangers, Cluster Flowered 'Purple Tiger' is an extraordinary variety best grouped with silver-leaved Artemisia 'Powis Castle'.

RIGHT: Bicoloured roses have special appeal. When cutting these and other varieties, plunge them to their necks in a bucket of water for a day, before arranging them.

ROSEMARY
Rosmarinus

An aromatic shrub and herb, rosemary embellishes a bed, border or patio tub with spires of blue, pink or white flowers in mid-spring.

Exploit the beauty of prostrate varieties by planting them to soften a hard corner or spill over a retaining wall.

FEATURES

Grown for its aromatic, evergreen foliage, *Rosmarinus officinalis* – there is only one species – embraces varieties with hooded, blue, pale violet, pink or white flowers in April and May. There are upright kinds to 1.8m (6ft) and compact, ground-covering forms to 60cm (2ft) across. Rosemary also makes a fetching, informal hedge.

Plant it to enhance a mixed shrub and perennial border, or in patio pots. If possible, position it where you will brush against it and detect its pleasing aroma. It is long-lived, matures within 3–5 years and flowers early in life. Rosemary, also a culinary herb, symbolises remembrance, love and fidelity.

CONDITIONS

Aspect	Rosemary, which must have full sun to develop stocky, free-flowering shoots, prospers in exposed inland and coastal gardens.
Site	Preferring well-drained, poor, sandy or gravelly soils, it abhors heavy clay.

GROWING METHOD

Feeding	Apart from working bone meal into the planting hole, no further fertiliser is usually necessary to ensure that rosemary flourishes.
Propagation	This shrub is easily increased from semi-ripe cuttings taken from mid- to late summer.
Problems	It is seldom attacked by pests and diseases, but its roots are liable to rot in soggy clay.

PRUNING

Upright varieties and hedges:	Keep plants compact and full of young growth by trimming them fairly hard with shears when flowers fade in late spring.
Carpeters:	Prune unwanted shoots in spring.

ROSEMARY AT A GLANCE

A hardy, small-leaved, aromatic, upright or carpeting evergreen, with usually blue, spring flowers. Hardy to -10°C (14°F).

		RECOMMENDED VARIETIES
JAN	/	
FEB	/	'Aureus'
MAR	/	'Benenden Blue'
APR	flower, plant	'Corsicus Prostratus'
MAY	flower, plant	'Miss Jessopp's Upright'
JUN	prune, plant	Prostratus Group
JULY	plant	'Tuscan Blue'
AUG	plant	
SEPT	plant	
OCT	/	
NOV	/	
DEC	/	

COTTON LAVENDER
Santolina

Effectively mantling and silvering this border edge, the dwarf form of cotton lavender, Santolina chamaecyparissus nana, *is a hardy evergreen.*

An arresting succession of lemon-yellow flowers clothe Santolina rosmarinifolia's *feathery, deep green stems from June to August.*

FEATURES

Mound forming, evergreen and ideal for making a low hedge to divide a lawn from a path or to segregate open-plan gardens, cotton lavender is prized for its aromatic, feathery, silvery-white or grey foliage. There is also a green-leaved form.

If cotton lavender is left to mature, a wealth of button-like, yellow flowers appear from June to August. Flowers, however, tend to spoil its symmetry and give it a ragged look. If you prefer foliage to blooms, prune bushes hard each year.

It is a tough shrub and unaffected by salty winds, so makes a good seaside plant. It also has few enemies.

Widely planted *Santolina chamecyparissus*, grows to around 45cm (18in) high and 75cm (30in) across and is favoured for hedging or punctuating a border. Its dwarf form, *nana*, just 30cm (12in) high, is fetching for edging a border or highlighting a rock garden.

Even whiter and more feathery is *S. pinnata neopolitana*, to 80cm (32in) high.

Equally decorative but with thread-like, green leaves, *S. rosmarinifolia* (*virens*) is massed with long-stemmed, yellow flowers in summer.

CONDITIONS

Aspect   Santolina is very hardy and braves low temperatures. Provided you set plants in full sun, where silvery-white-leaved varieties develop full radiance, they will excel for you. The green-leaved species tolerates light shade.

Site   This shrub performs zestfully on sandy loam but abhors heavy clay, which becomes soggy and airless in winter. If you are stuck with heavy clay, drain it by working in grit and channelling a gravel-lined drainage trench to a soakaway.

GROWING METHOD

Feeding   There is little need to be diligent with feeding, for cotton lavender prospers on thin and nutrient-sparse soils. However, lush growth will please you if in spring and autumn you work a dressing of bone meal into the root area.

Propagation   Increase your favourites from semi-ripe cuttings taken from early to mid-autumn and rooted in a garden frame or multiply plants from hardwood cuttings in late autumn.

Problems   Normally trouble free.

PRUNING

Shear off faded blooms in late August. Periodically – every 3 years or so when lower shoots are becoming woody – shorten stems to 15cm (6in) from the base to stimulate new basal growth.

COTTON LAVENDER AT A GLANCE

Evergreen bush with ferny or thread-like leaves and yellow, 'button' flowers from June to August. Hardy to -10°C (14°F).

		RECOMMENDED VARIETIES
JAN	/	
FEB	/	*S. chamaecyparissus*
MAR	/	*S. chamaecyparissus nana*
APR	plant, prune	*S. pinnata neopolitana*
MAY	plant, prune	*S. virens*
JUN	flower, plant	
JULY	flower, plant	
AUG	flower, plant	
SEPT	flower, plant	
OCT	/	
NOV	/	
DEC	/	

CHRISTMAS BOX
Sarcococca

Vanilla scent from the tiny flowers of Sarcococca hookeriana digyna, *a suckering evergreen to 1.8m (6ft), can waft for yards.*

Glossy leaved and smothered with scented, white blooms in winter, undemanding Sarcococca confusa *thrives in light shade.*

FEATURES

An easy, suckering, lance- or oval-leaved evergreen, sarcococca is a delight in February when tufted flowers of white or creamy male petals and smaller female blooms sleeve stems and release rich vanilla fragrance.

On a warm, breezy day, scent is detectable many yards from the bush. If you plant a group of it beneath a living-room window, the perfume will waft indoors. Cut blooms will scent a room.

Carpeting thickly and suppressing weeds, *Sarcococca hookeriana* forms a 30cm (12in) high thicket, 90cm (3ft) across. *Digyna*, a form of *S. hookeriana*, has purple-tinged leaves and thrusts to 1.2m (4ft). Its flowers are followed by black berries. Resembling privet, *S. confusa* is a neater version, to 75cm (2.5ft). Appealingly different, *S. ruscifolia* forms a rugged bush of broader leaves, to 90cm (3ft) high and across, and blooms are followed by red berries.

CONDITIONS

Aspect
Ideal for clothing dappled shady areas beneath trees or borders on the north side of a wall or fence and between houses, it prospers in full sun, too. Avoid deeply shaded sites where growth is less compact and flowering inhibited.

Site
Sarcococca favours deep, humus- and nutrient-rich, acid or alkaline soils that drain freely. Improve poor, sandy patches by working in bulky organic manure. Lighten and aerate heavy clay by digging in some grit or pea shingle.

Plant it in a large tub or pot to perfume a patio or terrace in mild spells during winter. Alternatively, set it to flank a path or driveway where you will brush against it and enjoy its 'clean', rich scent.

GROWING METHOD

Feeding
Encourage robust growth by working bone meal into the planting hole and pricking it into the root area in spring and autumn. Help young plants establish quickly by watering copiously after planting and in dry spells in their first year.

Propagation
Increase your stock by using a spade to slice off rooted suckers in spring or take semi-ripe cuttings of new shoots in midsummer.

Problems
Small, young plants may take several months to settle down and grow enthusiastically. Encourage them to develop quickly by liquid feeding fortnightly with a high-nitrogen fertiliser in spring and summer.

PRUNING

No regular cutting back is necessary. Remove dead or damaged shoots in spring.

CHRISTMAS BOX AT A GLANCE

White-flowered and sweetly scented, bushy or carpeting evergreen for sunny or lightly shaded places. Hardy to -15°C (4°F).

Month		RECOMMENDED VARIETIES
JAN	/	
FEB	flower	*S. confusa*
MAR	plant	*S. hookeriana digyna*
APR	plant, prune	*S. hookeriana humilis*
MAY	plant	*S. ruscifolia*
JUN	/	
JULY	/	
AUG	plant	
SEPT	plant	
OCT	/	
NOV	/	
DEC	/	

SPIRAEA
Spiraea

Transforming mid-spring with a fountain of snowy blossom on arching stems to 1.8m (6ft), bridal wreath (Spiraea arguta) is magnificent.

Unusually, late summer-flowering Spiraea 'Shirobana' yields a mix of mushroom-headed, white and rose-purple flowers.

FEATURES

An easy and floriferous family of deciduous shrubs, 45cm–2.4m (18in–8ft) high, spiraea rewards us with cone- or dome-shaped blooms on upright shoots or on pendulous or arching stems. There are two groups: spring flowering and summer flowering.

The finest early performers, from April to May, are epitomised by the aptly named bridal wreath (*Spiraea arguta*). Its arching stems, to 1.8m (6ft), are so thickly enveloped with snowy blossom that its leaves are concealed. Most popular summer-flowering members are forms of *S. japonica*: 'Anthony Waterer', aglow with domes of carmine-pink flowers amid pink or cream-tinged leaves; and 'Goldflame', prized for its dark pink flowers and radiant golden-orange leaves in spring. Another kind, *S. billiardii* 'Triumphans', is ablaze with rose-purple flower cones in July and August.

Plant spiraea to punctuate a border, carpet a rock garden pocket, adorn a patio tub or screen out an ugly view.

CONDITIONS

Aspect   Very hardy, these shrubs prefer full sun in which stocky shoots flower well and coloured-leaved varieties develop vivid hues.

Site   They also thrive in a wide range of well-drained soils but dislike dry or very alkaline conditions. Improve sandy patches by digging in plenty of rotted organic matter.

GROWING METHOD

Feeding   Encourage robust growth by gently working bone meal into the root area in spring and autumn. Help new plants recover quickly from transplanting by watering liberally and mulching in dry spells in spring and summer.

Propagation   Take soft-tip cuttings in early summer; semi-ripe cuttings from mid- to late summer; or hardwood cuttings in autumn. Some varieties can be divided or increased from suckers in early spring.

Problems   Control sap-sucking aphids, which colonise soft shoot tips, by spraying with pirimicarb, derris or horticultural soap.

PRUNING

Spring- and summer-flowering kinds that flower on older shoots: Cut out from the base one older stem in three when blooms fade. Summer-flowering varieties that bloom on the current-year shoots: Shorten all stems to 10cm (4in) from the base from early to mid-spring. Rejuvenate tall, old, woody varieties making little new growth by cutting all shoots to within 30cm (12in) of the base in early spring.

SPIRAEA AT A GLANCE	
Spring- or summer-flowering shrubs with white, pink or purple-rose blooms. Some have orange foliage. Hardy to -25ºC (-13ºF).	
JAN /	RECOMMENDED VARIETIES
FEB /	
MAR plant	Spring flowering
APR prune, flower	*S. arguta*
MAY flower, prune	*S. thunbergii*
JUN flower, plant	'Snowmound'
JULY flower, plant	Summer flowering
AUG flower, plant	'Anthony Waterer'
SEPT flower, plant	*S. x billiardii*
OCT plant	'Gold Mound'
NOV plant	'Little Princess'
DEC /	'Triumphans'

LILAC
Syringa

Fragrant trusses of lilac blossom are a spring highlight. Syringa vulgaris *varieties bloom best in an open, sunny position.*

Cottage-garden pleasure: this white 'Mme Lemoine' lilac has been skillfully pruned to form a globe of blossom in mid-May.

FEATURES

A vast and fragrant, deciduous family from S.E. Europe to E. Asia, its cone or plume-like flowers light up May and June. Most popular are varieties of *Syringa vulgaris*. Enchanting, double-flowered forms are mauve-pink 'Belle de Nancy', dark purple 'Charles Joly' and violet-red 'Paul Hariot'. Captivating singles include white 'Maud Notcutt' and creamy-yellow 'Primrose'. All make upright focal points to 2.4–3m (8–10ft).

The Canadian Hybrids – rose-hued 'Bellicent' and pale lilac 'Elinor' – tolerate shade better than *S. vulgaris* and bear plumy blossom. Accommodating dwarf varieties, to 1.2m (4ft), for small gardens or rockeries, are lilac-pink *S. meyeri* 'Palibin' and *S. pubescens* 'Superba'.

LILAC AT A GLANCE

Perfumed, cone- or plume-shaped blooms in many shades appear in spring. Hardiness rating according to species.

		RECOMMENDED VARIETIES
JAN	/	
FEB	/	*S. pubescens* 'Miss Kim'
MAR	plant	*S. pubescens* 'Superba'
APR	plant	*S. vulgaris* 'Belle de Nancy'
MAY	flower, plant	*S. vulgaris* 'Charles Joly'
JUN	flower, plant	*S. vulgaris* 'Mme Lemoine'
JULY	plant, prune	*S. vulgaris* 'Mrs Edward Harding'
AUG	plant	*S. vulgaris* 'Primrose'
SEPT	plant	*S. x prestoniae* 'Elinor'
OCT	plant	
NOV	plant, prune	
DEC	prune	

CONDITIONS

Aspect Lilac flowers best in full sun but tolerates light shade. Choose an open site, protected from strong drying winds, where air circulates freely, to reduce risk of leaves becoming mildewed.

Site These shrubs need well-drained, organically rich soil. Avoid chalky spots, which may cause lime-induced chlorosis, when leaves turn creamy yellow and die.

GROWING METHOD

Feeding Apply a complete plant food, such as Growmore or fish, blood and bone meal in spring and midsummer.

Propagation Commercially, varieties are usually budded or grafted on to privet rootstock. Alternatively, take soft-tip cuttings in early summer or semi-ripe cuttings from mid- to late summer.

Problems Lilac blight, characterised by angular, brown spots, destroys leaves and buds. There are no chemical controls so cut back affected shoots to healthy, white tissue and burn prunings. When mildew strikes, leaves are felted with powdery-white mould. Improve air flow by thinning crowded shoots and spraying with carbendazim, mancozeb or sulphur when symptoms appear.

PRUNING

Cut out spent flowers when petals fade. Keep bushes youthful and blooming freely by pruning out a quarter of the older shoots each year in winter. Remove basal suckers.

VIBURNUM
Viburnum

Horizontally-tiered Viburnum plicatum *'Mariesii' displays its large, lacy, sterile blossoms embracing small, fertile flowers in spring.*

A spring star is Viburnum x burkwoodii, *whose multitude of orb-shaped, pinkish-white blooms spill rich vanilla scent into the air.*

FEATURES

Coveted for their blossom, berries, foliage and architectural habit, deciduous and evergreen viburnums have year-round appeal. Flowers – clusters, globes and sprays – in pink or white, thickly clothe shoots. Most varieties are sweetly perfumed. Growing 75cm–3m (30in–10ft) or more, most species and varieties bloom within three years of planting. All make fetching statements: such as evergreen *Viburnum tinu*s, which also makes a dense, winter-flowering hedge; carpeting *V. davidii*, whose female plants are studded with turquoise-blue berries; *V carlesii*, studded with vanilla-scented, whitish-pink orbs in spring; and *V. x bodnantense* 'Dawn', clustered with rose-pink flowers from October to March.

VIBURNUM AT A GLANCE

Light up winter to summer with showy flowers and autumn with spectacular, scarlet berries. Hardiness according to species.

JAN	flower	RECOMMENDED VARIETIES
FEB	flower	
MAR	plant, flower	Winter flowering
APR	flower, prune	'Dawn'
MAY	flower, plant	'Deben'
JUN	flower, plant	*V. x bodnantense*
JULY	plant, prune	Spring flowering
AUG	plant	*V. carlesii* 'Aurora'
SEPT	plant	*V. x carlcephalum*
OCT	plant	*V. x opulus* 'Roseum'
NOV	plant	Autumn berrying
DEC	/	*V. betulifolium*
		V. davidii

CONDITIONS

Aspect Viburnums need at least half a day's full sunshine to prosper. Shield large-flowering varieties from chilly wind.

Site These shrubs prefer well-drained soil enriched with well-rotted organic matter several weeks before planting.
In light soils that parch quickly, mulch in spring with moisture-conserving, bulky organics to keep roots cool and active.

GROWING METHOD

Feeding Nourish growth by applying a balanced fertiliser, such as Growmore, chicken pellets or blood, fish and bone meal, in spring and midsummer. In a cold spring, boost growth of young plants by foliar feeding fortnightly with a high-potash fertiliser.
Water frequently newly planted viburnums in warm, dry weather.

Propagation Take soft-tip cuttings in spring; semi-ripe cuttings from mid- to late summer; and hardwood cuttings in late autumn. Layer shoots from mid-spring to late summer.

Problems Tackle viburnum beetle, which shreds leaves in summer, by spraying in late spring with permethrin, bifenthrin or pyrethrum.

PRUNING

V. tinus: Trim shoots lightly in early spring. Deciduous, winter-flowering species: Remove one stem in three every 2–3 years in spring. Evergreens: Cut out one stem in three, in midsummer, every four years.

WEIGELA
Weigela

Weigela florida *'Variegata' brightens late spring with a generous confection of pinkish blossom on year-old shoots.*

Compact and low growing, so ideal for small gardens, Weigela *'Rumba's shoots are thickly sleeved with radiant blooms.*

FEATURES

Flowering unstintingly from May to June, weigela is a reliable, hardy, deciduous shrub. Growing 1.2–1.8m (4–6ft) high and across, there are two main divisions: varieties of *Weigela florida* and a range of hybrids.
Two of the showiest forms of *W. florida* are dark purple-leaved and rose-pink-flowered 'Foliis Purpureis' and widely grown 'Variegata', whose green-and-yellow foliage complements pale pink blooms.
Appealing hybrids include 'Briant Rubidor', where golden-yellow to green leaves combine pleasingly with a wealth of vibrant, ruby-red flowers. Very different is *W*. 'Looymansii Aurea', which must be grown in light shade or its leaves, bright gold in spring, will scorch.

CONDITIONS

Aspect	Most varieties flower best if planted in full sun. Shield them from strong wind, too, which can damage flowers and 'burn' soft, new leaves.
Site	Encourage vigorous growth by setting plants in well-drained soil, including chalk, enriched with plenty of well-decayed manure.

GROWING METHOD

Feeding	Boost sturdy shoots sleeved with blossom by topdressing the root area with bone meal in spring and autumn and mulching in spring.
Propagation	Take soft-tip cuttings in early summer; semi-ripe cuttings from mid- to late summer; and hardwood cuttings in autumn.
Problems	Pale green capsid bugs, about 6mm (¼in) long, suck sap from shoot tips and secrete a toxin that kills cells. When leaves unfold, damaged areas become ragged holes. Control by spraying with pirimiphos-methyl or fenitrothion when symptoms seen.

PRUNING

Keep bushes young and packed with blossom by removing from the base one in three of the oldest flowering stems when blooms fade.

WEIGELA AT A GLANCE

Bushy shrubs bearing trumpet-shaped, white, pink, red or purple-red blooms from May to June. Hardy to -25°C (-13°F).

JAN	/	RECOMMENDED VARIETIES
FEB	/	'Abel Carriere'
MAR	plant	'Briant Rubidor'
APR	plant	'Carnival'
MAY	flower, plant	'Foliis Purpureis'
JUN	flower, plant	*W. middendorffiana*
JULY	prune, plant	'Newport Red'
AUG	plant	'Rumba'
SEPT	plant	'Variegata'
OCT	plant	
NOV	plant	
DEC	/	

WISTERIA
Wisteria

Trained to cover a warm, sunny wall, Chinese wisteria (Wisteria sinensis) yields fragrant, lilac-blue to white flowers in May and June.

Festooned with chunky blooms in late spring, Wisteria brachybotrys is also called silky wisteria because of its softly hairy leaves.

FEATURES

Wisteria takes the accolade for cloaking beautifully in May and June a wall, fence, pergola, arch or tree. Taking 3–4 years to establish and flowering freely, its long chains of pea-like blooms cascade from woody spurs. Blossoms on some varieties are followed by attractive, runner bean-like seed pods.

Buy only grafted plants – look for a bulge where scion and stock unite – because seedlings can take many years to flower and often they do not do so at all.

If space is limited, this handsome, twining, deciduous climber can be planted in a large patio tub and trained as a standard, to around 2.4m (8ft) high.

Choice kinds are sweetly scented Chinese wisteria (*Wisteria sinensis*), which displays lilac-blue to white flowers. Its varieties – white 'Alba' and deep violet-blue 'Caroline' – are spectacular. The silky wisteria (*W. brachybotrys*) has softly hairy, pinnate leaves, which complement shortish, yellow-blotched, violet to white blooms. The stunning Japanese wisteria (*W. floribunda* 'Alba') treats us to clusters of white blossom, which extend impressively to 60cm (2ft) long.

CONDITIONS

Aspect   A sheltered, sunny or very lightly shaded, south- or west-facing position is essential for flowering. For unless new shoots are exposed daily to many hours of sunlight or to bright incidental light, they may not ripen sufficiently for flowers to form.

Site   Virtually any well-drained soil – the more fertile the better – suits this rampant climber. Chalky, alkaline soil may inhibit the uptake of iron vital for chlorophyll formation and cause leaves to become weak and creamy green.

GROWING METHOD

Feeding   A spring and autumn application of bone meal encourages robust growth. Mulch with bulky organic materials to conserve moisture.

If, despite regular pruning, flowers fail to form, topdress the root area with 28g per sq m (1oz per sq yd) of shoot-ripening sulphate of potash in February.

Propagation   Layer shoots from mid-spring to late summer or root soft-tip cuttings in a mist propagation unit in midsummer.

Problems   Reluctance to flower can be due to planting a seedling, insufficient light or not pruning.

PRUNING

In July, shorten to five compound leaves new shoots springing from the main branches. In November, reduce shortened shoots to two buds to encourage flowering spurs to form.

WISTERIA AT A GLANCE

Spring-flowering climber laden with chains of pea flowers, for warm, sunny walls, fences and trees. Hardy to -15°C (4°F).

Month	Activity	Recommended Varieties
JAN	/	
FEB	/	*W. brachybotrys*
MAR	plant	*W. floribunda* 'Alba'
APR	plant	*W. sinensis*
MAY	plant, flower	*W. sinensis* 'Alba'
JUN	plant, flower	*W. sinensis* 'Caroline'
JULY	prune	
AUG	plant	
SEPT	plant	
OCT	/	
NOV	prune	
DEC	/	

FLOWERING CHART

PLANT NAME	SPRING			SUMMER			AUTUMN			WINTER		
	EARLY	MID	LATE	EARLY	MID	LATE	EARLY	MID	LATE	EARLY	MID	LATE
Abelia					❀	❀	❀					
Abutilon				❀	❀							
Acacia		❀										
Ardisia					❀	❀						
Berberis		❀	❀									
Buddleja				❀	❀	❀						
Buxus		❀		❀								
Callistemon				❀	❀							
Camellia	❀	❀							❀	❀	❀	❀
Ceanothus			❀	❀	❀	❀	❀	❀				
Chaenomeles	❀	❀	❀	❀								
Choisya		❀	❀				❀					
Cistus			❀	❀	❀							
Convolvulus cneorum			❀	❀	❀							
Cornus	❀		❀	❀		❀						❀
Cotinus				❀	❀							
Cotoneaster			❀	❀								
Crataegus			❀	❀								
Cytisus			❀	❀								
Daphne	❀	❀	❀	❀								
Deutzia			❀	❀	❀							
Echium				❀	❀	❀	❀					
Erica	❀	❀	❀	❀	❀	❀	❀	❀	❀	❀	❀	❀
Escallonia				❀	❀	❀	❀					
Euphorbia		❀	❀	❀								
Fatsia								❀	❀			
Forsythia	❀	❀										
Genista			❀	❀	❀	❀						
Hamamelis										❀	❀	❀
Hebe			❀	❀	❀	❀	❀	❀				
Helianthemum				❀	❀	❀						

PLANT NAME	SPRING			SUMMER			AUTUMN			WINTER		
	EARLY	MID	LATE	EARLY	MID	LATE	EARLY	MID	LATE	EARLY	MID	LATE
Heliotropium				✿	✿	✿	✿	✿	✿	✿	✿	
Hibiscus				✿	✿		✿					
Hydrangea				✿	✿		✿					
Jasminum			✿	✿	✿	✿	✿				✿	✿
Kerria		✿	✿									
Lavandula					✿	✿	✿					
Leptospermum			✿	✿	✿							
Lonicera		✿	✿	✿	✿	✿	✿				✿	✿
Magnolia	✿	✿	✿		✿	✿	✿					
Mahonia	✿	✿									✿	✿
Nandina				✿	✿	✿						
Nerium			✿	✿	✿	✿	✿	✿	✿	✿		
Osmanthus		✿	✿				✿	✿				
Philadelphus				✿	✿							
Photinia		✿	✿	✿								
Pieris	✿	✿	✿									
Potentilla			✿	✿	✿	✿	✿	✿				
Plumbago					✿	✿	✿	✿				
Prunus	✿	✿	✿	✿								
Punica				✿	✿	✿						
Pyracantha				✿								
Rhododendron	✿	✿	✿	✿	✿							✿
Ribes		✿	✿									
Rosa		✿	✿	✿	✿	✿	✿	✿				
Rosmarinus		✿	✿									
Santolina				✿	✿	✿						
Sarcococca												✿
Syringa			✿	✿								
Viburnum		✿	✿	✿							✿	✿
Weigela			✿	✿							✿	
Wisteria			✿	✿								

INDEX

INDEX

Published by Murdoch Books UK Ltd, 1999
Ferry House, 51-57 Lacy Road, Putney, London SW15 1PR

This edition published 2001 for INDEX: Henson Way,
Kettering, NN16 8PX, United Kingdom

First published 1999. This edition published 2001. Printed by Toppan in China.

ISBN 1-897730-76-4

COMMISSIONING EDITOR: Helen Griffin

SERIES EDITOR: Graham Strong

TEXT: John Negus and Margaret Hanks

ILLUSTRATIONS: Matthew Ottley

DESIGNERS: Bill Mason and Annette Fitzgerald

PUBLISHER: Anne Wilson

PHOTOGRAPHS: All photographs by Lorna Rose except those by Ed Gabriel: pp 11(L), 12(L), 14(L), 16,
23(L), 24, 28(R), 30(L and R), 33(L and R), 38, 39(R), 41, 42(L), 44(L and R), 51, 52(L),
55, 57(R), 59, 63(R), 65(R), 70, 79(L and R), 85(L and R), 86(L), 87(L and R), 90(L), 91(R), back cover.
Neil Holmes, Garden Picture Library: p 67(L);
Stirling Macoboy: pp 15(R), 53(L), 35(R);
John Negus: pp 57(L), 67(R);
Eric Sawford: p 45(R);
Derek St. Romaine: p45(L);
and Harry Smith Collection: pp 11(R), 12(R), 18(R), 29(R), 31(R), 42(R), 48(R), 52(R), 62(R), 63(L), 86(R), 90(R).

FRONT COVER: Blue hydrangeas
TITLE PAGE: Delicate and fragrant: a double form of *Camellia saluensis*